CURRICULUM STUDIES

COMPETENCE-BASED CURRICULUM DEVELOPMENT IN HIGHER EDUCATION

DR. MUKTA GOYAL MR. UDAY MODAK

Copyright © Dr. Mukta Goyal Mr. Uday Modak
All Rights Reserved.

This book has been published with all efforts taken to make the material error-free after the consent of the author. However, the author and the publisher do not assume and hereby disclaim any liability to any party for any loss, damage, or disruption caused by errors or omissions, whether such errors or omissions result from negligence, accident, or any other cause.

While every effort has been made to avoid any mistake or omission, this publication is being sold on the condition and understanding that neither the author nor the publishers or printers would be liable in any manner to any person by reason of any mistake or omission in this publication or for any action taken or omitted to be taken or advice rendered or accepted on the basis of this work. For any defect in printing or binding the publishers will be liable only to replace the defective copy by another copy of this work then available.

Contents

Contents

Foreword

I am delighted and honoured to write the foreword of the Edited Book "**Curriculum Studies: Competency-based Curriculum Development in Higher Education**". I must congratulate the endeavor of two experienced teachers in their respective fields. I believe that teachers at every level and stage of their career can enrich and strengthen their teaching by learning the discussion-leading patterns and practices presented in this book. Participating in interpretive discussions can help teachers and students alike learn to use their minds with power and pleasure.

This book resonates with the key themes in different areas of Curriculum Studies that is helpful for the readers to have a clear picture of the specific subjects. The framework annotated examples, and appendixes can structure and guide teachers' joint work as they prepare questions, co-lead discussions, observe and analyze classroom experiments, and discuss emergent questions and problems. As teachers gain confidence and skill through collaborative experimentation and development, they can also study the impact of participating in such discussions on students' confidence and academic skills.

I wish this Edited Book a grand success. The present edited volume will be useful for research scholars, social science researchers, teachers, teacher educators, and professional developers, helping teachers across the country to learn, teach, and practice the art of interpretive discussion. I also wish that the Editors take this initiative again to bring about a change and progress of the society through their great concern and measure.

Dr Savita Mishra
Principal
Vidyasagar College of Education, Phansidewa
Darjeeling, West Bengal

Message

It gives me immense pleasure to announce the launch of a new publication titled **"Curriculum Studies: Competency-Based Curriculum Development in Higher Education"** edited by Dr. Mukta Goyal and Mr. Uday Modak who are having experience as working professional and also experienced educator shares with us the significance of skill development for any career one opts for, which is guided by their lifelong research and hard work through this exceptional publication. I congratulate them for their sheer hard work on this exemplary accomplishment.

(DR. RAJAT DEY)

Principal,
Bhavan's Tripura College of Teacher Education,
Narsingarh , Agartala, Tripura.

Preface

Over the last decade, novel trends in higher education have seen the emergence of innovative learning initiatives involving the application of new technologies and emerging technology tools, as well as delivery platforms and new business model pedagogy. Competency-based education (CBE) is one such initiative that has become one of the most popular "buzzwords" in academia today.

A curriculum is more than just a syllabus or a list of course materials. A curriculum is about what should happen in a teaching program—what teachers intend to do and how they intend to do it. In order to plan and develop a meaningful curriculum, faculty must closely examine and analyse the various forces that provide direction for curriculum changes. Curriculum development refers to all of the methods that a training or teaching institution uses to plan and guide understanding. This learning can take place in groups or individually with students. It can happen inside or outside of the classroom. A curriculum is a well-designed framework for the teaching and learning process. It contains learning objectives that students must be aware of. When students are aware of the learning objectives, they can plan, execute, and evaluate them in order to achieve the course learning outcome. A well-designed curriculum comes with the resources necessary to supplement it. These resources include, among other things, experiment ideas, learning activities, projects, assignments, and references. These resources are critical for both teachers and students.

The book entitled **"Curriculum Studies: Competence-Based Curriculum Development in Higher Education"** is a product of our long experience as a teacher in a College, Department of Education. As a teacher, we felt a new interest in them and this led us to take this laborious and ambitious venture. In writing this book we have always kept in mind the interest of the students who will primarily be benefited by it. Educators and general readers may also get valuable information regarding the theories and practices of the Emerging Trends in Higher Education all over world.

The urgent need of students studying in B.Ed, M.Ed, and B.A (Ed), M.A (Ed) classes and UGC NET, SET, SLET, (Ed) examination preparation purposes together with the continuous persuasion of May worthy friends inspired. Certainly, there is no such book that deals with the **"Curriculum Studies: Competence-Based Curriculum Development in Higher**

Education" presents healthy solutions of all the conflicting educational problems according to the syllabus of all the universities of the country. We are confident that this book fulfills all essential requirements and its wide circulation will definitely exert an important influence on the theory of Education.

The curriculum, in addition to creating shared goals between teachers and students, standardizes learning goals for an entire organization and provides a clear path for students to progress from one grade to the next. Before moving on to more advanced subjects, students must master certain core competencies, such as algebra before attempting calculus. Knowledge is like a glue that holds information and learning together. We understand a topic better when we have prior knowledge of it. It is very important in the lives of students, especially in school. They will struggle to understand the text if they do not have relevant knowledge. Without such a standardized curriculum and instruction, with this knowledge in place, instructors would have to develop their own learning objectives and collaborate in some way to ensure that their students are on track.

Our Indian society has transformed from medieval and traditional to modern pattern. Thus society can survive only if there exists among its members a sufficient degree of homogeneity.

In completing this self-imposed stupendous task, the authors have been quite conscious of their numerous limitations in view of the multifarious subject matter to be collected for completing this volume. At various junctures, we have been necessarily very short, but we have seen that no basic ideas and essentials of any educator are overlooked. In a work of this nature, it will be preposterous on the part of the authors to claim any originality. However, in making certain evaluations of some Emerging Trends in Higher Education chosen for discussion in this book, the authors have frankly expressed their convictions. It is hoped that these will merit the attention of the readers.

This book will also assist students in understanding the fundamentals of the curriculum, including its concepts, principles, phases, and models.

In addition, the current book aims to provide a comprehensive analysis of the most recent trends and issues that curriculum developers and users must consider when developing relevant and interesting curricula.

Dr.Mukta Goyal
Mr. Uday Modak

CHAPTER I

Curriculum Studies

**Mr. Bhanumoorthy K

• • •

Abstract

The word curriculum is derived from the Latin word "currere" – means a race course or run way on which one runs to reach a goal. It is an educative programme by which pupils achieve goals and aspirations of life. As per dictionary, means the subjects included in a course of study both academic and non-academic activities. we are fully aware that our nation is unity under diversity. India is a union of 28-states and 8 union territories. State Governments do prepare their own curriculum of course, following the guiding principles of the of national policy on education. They make their own assessment system, evaluation scheme. In social science, the contents are based on the important aspects of the respective states where the students are supposed to know and to be familiar, be known to students. Another valid aspect is we have different boards, namely CBSE, ICSE, matriculation. They make their own curriculum. However, guide lines on national educational policy are adhered to, with respect to course of study. Different people define the word curriculum in different ways. To quote, Mr. Cunningham says, "It is a tool in the hands of a teacher who moulds students with respect to aims and objectives. Mr. Morroe says, "activities carried out to attain aims of education. "Mr. Crow and Crow says, "a student's development, in emotion stability, spiritually upright, morally sound and social mobility." Up to 1970, Education has been largely a state subject, but by 42nd amendment it has come in the concurrent list. Since independence India adopted national educational policy (NPE) 1968,1986,1992. Now present 2020 NPE.

"The curriculum of the school did not neglect India's cultural, analytical and scientific heritage, but was very involved also with the rest of the world." ----- **Amartya Sen.**

Keywords: aims, objectives, unity, diversity, mould, development, culture, heritage.

Introduction:

"If we teach today as we taught yesterday, then we rob our children of tomorrow." ----- **John Dewey.**

There were many education commissions. The main thrust was quality education to everyone, development of society where does one live in. The commissions were for university education, Secondary education, teacher education, universalization of elementary education. These commissions recommended and also focused, on systematic change in the system. National curriculum Frame work (NCFW)2005 recommended to reduce work load on elementary education .to learn without tension, to provide experiences to children and attain language skills. In the year 1961 NCERT was formed an autonomous body to give guide lines to both union and state governments on formulating education policies.

Curriculum is the totality of experience that pupils receive through the manifold activities that go in the school, in the class room, library, laboratories, workshop playground and in numerous contacts between teachers and students.

Understanding the meaning:

It comprises a set of lessons and academic content taught in a school or in a specific course or program. Curriculum is an important element of education, aims are reflected in, determined by the aims of life and society. As time pass by, aims are subject to lots of changes as and when required. Aims of education are attained by school program or any institution program, skills to be acquired, activities to be carried out, knowledge to acquire. Curriculum is a set of instructional strategies; the students achieve goals. It centres around two aspects. 1. Development of an individual. 2. To understand the immediate neighbourhood where he/she lives in. We as human beings have lots of potential, they are to be moulded through a chain of changes. This kind of periodic changes, prepare, empower the leaders, teaching fraternity, to know the latest teaching -learning process/methods enabling students' community (the present generation) raise up with more confident, meet the challenges.

A quote by **Heather Casey:**

"There is no set curriculum. Every child, every parent is different, but this program gives parents the tools to start the learning process."

Components of Curriculum:

"The ocean of knowledge is profound and deeper you dive, the more insight you will gain from it." ----- **Shivanshu K Srivastava.**

The components are

1. Communication Arts

Under this heading we prepare students to attain the specific skills in language namely listening, speaking, reading, writing, how to use the language with correct pronunciation, proper intonation, speaking with appropriate word group, mean to say where to put a pause and continue to speak.

1. Mathematics:

It is a very interesting subject, prepare the students, for reasoning, logical thinking. In fact, it is used in our daily life. Under the subject we do teach numeric, various skills, Geometry, Algebra, Logic.

3. Science:

We do concentrate on all branches of natural sciences. (Physics, chemistry, botany, zoology) There are various topics in every branch, the level of contents according to every class is taken care.

4. Social Science:

In this subject we have sub-division such as history, geography, civics. We have Indian history, World history, civilization, ancient history, Indian Constitution, rules and regulations, Fundamental duties and rights, how the Government functions, Powers of President, prime Minister, district authorities, their powers, Judiciary, Regional, local level administration. Geography furnishes with globes, World Indian maps, earth and planets, solar system, weather, rainfall so on. The contents are taken care to the level of students in each branch.

5. Music:

We are fully aware the first activity of a school/ institution starts with a prayer, where mass singing takes place. Learning Music has an aesthetic value. Singing gives pleasure, joy. For music, language is not barrier. We prepare students not only in scholastic areas, in non-scholastic areas also. Of course, it is a part of curriculum.

6. Physical Education:

We prepare the students physically fit, healthy, a sound mind in a sound body. There is a provision in our curriculum to fulfil, attain our aims, objectives. Teachers are appointed to prepare the students in various games and sports. In a timetable, definitely there is a slot, shown the number of periods per week. An elaborate description is given in the syllabus. At school level, regional level, national level students are prepared to meet the challenges, encouraging them to participate.

7. Value education:

"The aim of education is knowledge, not of facts but of Values." ----- **William S Burroughs.**

Education is the preparation for one's life. In fact, education is, life itself. It is the modification of one's behavior. It has to be value oriented, not simply knowledge based. What values are to be inculcated during the course of schooling/academic career are clearly specified rather defined in a nutshell. There are aesthetic values, Spiritual values, Moral values, Social Values. All these values to be inculcated among students, these are finding their places in curriculum. They are essential for all round development of students. (Music, dance, drawing, painting, dance drama, mono act, mimicry) One has to spiritually balanced, morally upright, socially attached to the immediate society (neighborhood) as fellow being. Apart from that one has to be emotionally stable. Now a days we talk about Emotion quotient (EQ) apart from IQ.

8. We can add one more so to say Life skills:

A quote from **Billie Jean King.**

"I think self-awareness is probably the most important thing towards being a champion."

World health organization has given a list of Life skills, CBSE has listed out about 80 skills A school is a place where children are to be taught, to acquire life skills to lead the life happily and understand the very purpose of life. The system of education provides sufficient opportunities to make every one efficient.

Let us discuss objectives/Aims:

1. Objectives:

In every subject there are specific objectives. For example, in language the skills such as listening, reading, speaking and writing. Minimum level of learning is to be attained in every subject. In the prescribed textbook the contents are standardized. In curriculum why education should be provided, what has to be done towards the right direction, vividly given. In every lesson of every subject, skills to acquire are focused and spelt out. Learners' capacity, attitudes, and potential for learning, motivation, needs, interests and values are taken care.

2. Content:

What is to be taught and learnt, scope of the subject matters and in proper sequence is a matter of concern, to the level of students. The contents are graded. There is a vertical and horizontal integration from class to class. There is continuity so to say a chain of learning and linkage of other subjects too. There are some criteria. They are content has to be a) self-sufficient b) significant c) validity d) interest e) utility f) feasibility, in brief scope of the subject elaboration. Every academic year is split into three terms, the whole syllabus is divided with duration of time frame (hours of teaching). This would help teachers to prepare good lesson plans for teaching- learning process.

3. Learning experiences:

What are the instructional strategies /models of transaction of teaching-learning experiences? The different approaches, methods depending upon the topic are well expressed. (Methodology). Learning experiences both within in the institutions and outside. Learning environments with congenial atmosphere, providing teachers materials, to enhance effective teaching learning.

4. Evaluation:

Evaluation plays an important role in learning -teaching process. This would facilitate/ guides, students and teachers for effective learning and teaching. Evaluation is a continuous process. It is very necessary to know the status, progress and achievement of a child. At the same time, certainly it helps teachers, to guide the students who are not up to the mark, remedial measures to be under taken to enhance their academic performance. Techniques and methods to be used are very well detailed. Of course, it depends which board students do study. This kind of evaluation is periodical, students to move to next higher class with minimum level of learning. It goes without saying there lies the commitment and accountability of teachers.

Foundation of Curriculum:

1. **Philosophical:**

"Trust yourself. You know more than you think you do." ----- **Benjamin Spock.**

The contents are to be put across in an organized manner. Provision to be given for critical thinking, logical reasoning, taking decisions to proceed further in studies. Contents are concerned with guiding principles on aims of education, attitudes, beliefs of an individual, teaching leaning process in school environment. There are guiding principles, the relationship between teachers and students, the relationship of teachers with other colleagues, other members of school and also with authority. In this connection different philosophers define education in many ways, ultimately the main thrust on cognitive development, moral development, physical development and spiritual development and character development, to be humane in all aspects.

2. **Social:**

"Attitude is a little thing that makes a big difference." --**Winston Churchill.**

Definitely there is a kind of bond, relationship between curriculum and the society. We are attached with society or with immediate neighborhood, where do live in. One cannot live alone rather in aloof. The curriculum has direct influence on the society. Human beings are social animals if I am correct.

3. **Psychological:**

"A wonderful fact to reflect upon, that every human creature is constituted to be that of profound secret and mystery to every other." ---- **Charles Dickens.**

Teachers have to study and know the psychology of children, especially who teach primary classes. Schools are" home away from home" there is a saying. In that context I would say know the child and teach the child. Psychology provides basis for the teaching learning process. It is the scientific study of mental functions and one's behavior. The psychological approach helps an individual (student) modifies one's behavior, also learning is acquired at the optimum level.

Principles of Curriculum Construction:

The basic principles are forward looking, creative, preparation of life, linking with life. The principles are in consonance with the national and international demands /requirements. Curriculum provide opportunities/ situations/ occasions, to verify the activities carried out by students, both mentally and physically. It is also connected with our societal needs and the children interest are also paid attention in framing curriculum. Regional and national conditions are understood and considered. Practical utility for students' community is duly paid attention. Students shall be able to go in the opted direction and understand the principles of life and will be able to adjust and lead life happily. I would like to emphasis, suggest on these aspects too. To be child centered, need more experiences than mere instructions (to provide sufficient opportunities). Activities have to be related with child's educational requirements and desires. It is not simply collection of topics, the very philosophy /culture of a nation to be reflected. Apart from the above, it is essential learning has to be conceptual enabling students for retention, to discourage rote learning, to be skill oriented not knowledge based only. How learning linked with our daily life to be incorporated, helpful for self-employment. In a nutshell the wholesome personality of a child is developed. A sense of belongingness to one's nation, a befitting citizen of our nation, be a better human being, possess an excellent character. Understand the purpose of life, serve the nation.

Conclusion:

"Curriculum is a tool in the hands of the artist (teacher) to mould his/her, materials (students), according to his/her ideals (objectives) in his/her studio (college/school.)" ----- **Cunningham.**

Curriculum is the totality of experience that pupils receive through the manifold activities that go in the school, in the class room, library, laboratories, workshop, playground, in numerous informal contacts between teachers and students. This is need of the hours. Preparing curriculum is not that easy, it is a difficult task, takes time to incorporate, many aspects. The curriculum is being prepared, by a team of members, contributed by subject experts, eminent scholars, educationists, academicians. They do forecast the essential content matters, to meet the challenges, the days to come. What I studied in my graduation; present day students do study in secondary, senior secondary classes. So periodical change is a must. In this write up I have shared my experiences as a teacher and as a head of a school. Institutions are established to educate students, prepare them, acquire good character, the life skills, attain the set-in goals, be a good citizen of a nation and a better human being. Parents send their children with lots of aspirations, dreams for the sake of giving them the education as expected by them. It is not always easy to change a student's life, but a great teacher can do so. Students who are inspired by their teachers can accomplish amazing results, and that motivation always stays with them lifelong. So dear teachers let us raise up with team spirit, put one's optimum/maximum abilities, be efficient and effective teacher. I do take pride that I am a teacher. Let me conclude with a quote by Ernest Agyemang Yeboah.

"I stand for a different education: a different education where students will not just learn, but they will reproduce great and noble things with what learn."

References:

- *School View panel* by TS Bhujanga Rao.
- Online Resources

Jai Hind

CHAPTER II

Concept of Curriculum

**Barsha Debnath

• • •

Abstract:

Curriculum places an important role in an educational system or we can say curriculum is the heart of education process. It is somehow a blueprint which leads the teacher and the learner to reach the desired objectives. As a result authorities have to design it in such a way that it could lead the teacher and the learner meet the desired learning outcomes. Though the child's development and growth is the main consideration of curriculum construction yet his social behaviour is also to be suitably developed, both the individual development and the social development of the child deserve equal attention.

Curriculum framers should used practical approach rather than ideological, reorganizing of recent curricula, solving language issue, facing controversies on curriculum change, obtaining continuous feedback and developing hearing in society at the same time. It is imperative for scholars to have effective communication skills and dynamic personality to incorporate the future trends without creating conflicts and confusion in the society. They need to know the skill to motivate and mould high ups for future changes and bring changes without development of controversies.

Key words:

Curriculum, Education, Scholar, Communication skill.

Introduction:

Curriculum is the crux of the whole educational process. Without curriculum, we cannot conceive any educational Endeavour. • The curriculum in a literal sense, a pathway towards a goal. • Curriculum is actually what happens during a course i.e., lecture , demonstrations, field visits, the work with the client and so on. • Curriculum also means a written description of what happens.

▶ Curriculum is an important element of education. Aims of education are reflected in the curriculum. In other words, the curriculum is determined by the aims of life and society. Aims of life and society are subject to constant change.

▶ The term curriculum has been derived from a Latin word 'Currere' which means a 'race course' or a runway on which one runs to reach a goal. If the teacher is the guide, the curriculum is the path. Curriculum is the total structure of ideas and activities.

Meaning of Curriculum:

Curriculum is an important part of education. The term Curriculum has been derived from a Latin would "Currere" which means a 'race course' or a runway on which one runs to reach a goal. The term Curriculum refers to the lessons and academic content taught in a school or in a specific course or program.

It is curriculum through which the general aims of a school education receive Concrete expression. Curriculum is the total sum of all the activities and experiences provided by the institution to the learners for their all-around development and for achieving the goals of education.

Curriculum is a tool in the hands of artist (the teacher) to make his materials (the pupils) according to his ideal (objective) in his studio (the institution). Curriculum is not just written on page, but the curriculum is reflected in teachers'behaviour& conduct. Everything done in the institution to Curriculum like classroom instructions, students Activities, work experiences, school parties etc. Therefore, we can say - Curriculum in theheart of education process.

Components of Curriculum:

Curriculum plays an important role in an educational system. There are 4 basic components of curriculum and these are ----

a.   Curriculum objectives.
b.   Curriculum content or subject matter.
c.   Curriculum experience.
d.   Curriculum evaluation.

These four components of the curriculum are essential. These are interrelated to each other. Each of these has a connection to one another. I could say that these are essential ingredients to have an effective Curriculum.

a.   **Curriculum objectives:**

The Curriculum aims, goals and objectives spell-out what is to be done. It tries to capture what goals are to be achieved, the vision, the philosophy, the mission statement and objectives.Further, it clearly defines the purpose and what the curriculum is to be acted upon and try what to drive at.

There are four main factors affecting the formulation of curriculum objectives. These are—

i. The society.
ii. The knowledge.
iii. The learner.
iv. The learningprocesses.

All of these factors are to be considered while selecting and formulating the curriculum objectives.

a. **Curriculum content or subject matter:**

A second element is the content of the curriculum. It contains information to be learned in school. It is an element or a medium through which the objectives are accomplished.

One of the important considerationsis the selection of content for a subject. At the time of subject matter selection, the following factors are to be kept in mind:

a. Available sources and resources.
b. Demand of society
c. International needs.
d. Level and age of the learner or the student.
e. Methods of content organization.
f. Number of courses offered.
g. Scope of subject matter.
h. System of examination.
a. Quantity and qualification of teaching staff.

c. **Learning experiences (methods of delivering knowledge):**

The term "learning experiences" is not the same as the content with which course deals nor the activities performed by the teacher. The term "learning experience" refers to the interaction between the learner and the external condition in the environment to which he/she can react. Learning takes place through the active behaviour of the student.

d. Curriculum evaluation:

Curriculum evaluation is different from a student evaluation. It is a broader term being used to make a judgement about the worth and effectiveness of curriculum. Curriculum evaluation is also important in a sense that one could assess whether the aim and objectives have been met or not.

Foundation of curriculum:

Just as curriculum can be defined in a variety of ways, one can approach the evaluation and creation of curriculum through more than one foundational lens:

Philosophical, sociological and psychological. All three of this hold importance in influencing curriculum and instruction.

Philosophical Foundations: Philosophy lays the strong foundation of any curriculum. A curriculum planner or specialist, implementer or the teacher, school heads, evaluator anchors his/her decision-making process on a sound philosophy. Philosophy provides educators, teachers and curriculum makers with framework for planning, implementing and evaluating curriculum in school, answering what schools are for, what subjects are important, how students should learn and what materials and methods should be used. In decision-making, philosophy provides the starting point and will be used for the succeeding decision-making.

The following four educational philosophies relate to curriculum:

- **Perennialism:** The focus in the curriculum is classical subjects, literary analysis and considers curriculum as constant.
- **Essentialism:** The essential skills of the 3 R's and essential subjects of English, Science, History, Math and Foreign Language is the focus of the curriculum.
- **Progressivism:** The curriculum is focused on students' interest, human problems and affairs. The subjects are interdisciplinary, integrative and interactive.
- **Reconstructionism:** The focus of the curriculum is on present and future trends and issues of national and international interests.

Psychological Foundations: Curriculum is influenced by psychology. Psychology provides information about the teaching and learning process. It also seeks answers as to how a curriculum be organized in order to achieve students' learning at the optimum level, and as to what amount of information they can absorb in learning the various contents of the curriculum. Psychology provides basis for the teaching and learning process. It unifies elements of the learning process and some of the sum of questions which can be addressed by psychological foundation.

The following three are psychological theories in learning that influenced curriculum development:

Behaviourists Psychology: consider that learning should be organized in order that students can experience success in the process of mastering the subject matter, and thus, method of teaching should be introduced in a step-by-step manner with proper sequencing of task.

Cognitive Psychology: focus their attention on how individuals process information and how the monitor and manage thinking. For the cognitive theorists, learning constitutes a logical method for organizing and interpreting learning. Learning is rooted in the tradition of subject matter where teachers use a lot of problem and thinking skills in teaching learning. These are exemplified by practices like reflective thinking, creative thinking, intuitive thinking, discovery learning, etc.

Humanistic Psychology: Concerned with how learners can develop their human potential. Based on Gestalt psychology where learning can be explained in terms of the wholeness of the problem and where the environment is changing and the learner is continuously reorganizing his/her perceptions. Curriculum is concerned with the process the products, personal needs not subject matter; psychological meaning and environmental situations.

Socio-Cultural Foundations: Schools exists within the social context. Societal culture affects and shapes schools and their curricula. The relationship of curriculum and society is mutual and encompassing. Hence, to be relevant, the curricula should reflect and preserve the culture of society and its aspirations. At the same time, society should also imbibe the changes brought about by the formal institutions called schools. However, it is also imperative that a country must have maintained a curriculum that reflects and preserves its culture and aspirations for national identity. No matter how far people go, it is the country's responsibility to ensure that the school serves its purpose of educating the citizenry.

Principles of curriculum construction:
Curriculum is based on following important principles: -

1. **Principals of utility:**

Curriculum should be useful rather than decorative. The curriculum must have practical utility for students.

2. **Principle of child Centeredness:**

Curriculum should be child- centred. It should be based on the child's needs, interests, abilities, aptitude age level and circumstances.

Infact, curriculum is meant to bring about the development of the child in the desired direction so that he is able to adjust well in life.

3) Principle of community centeredness:
According to the curriculum growth and development of child is very important but his social behaviour is also to be suitably developed. He should understand member of the community and try to solve them in a systematic way as he is to live in and for the society. So, the values, attitudes and skills that are prevailing in the community must be reflected in curriculum.

4) Principles of activity centeredness:
Curriculum must be full of activities. As child learn maximum things from activities. It should be connected with the child's desires and needs. The useful activities both in the class room and outside the class room should be provided.

5) Principles of interrelation of subject:
Curriculum should be such that all the subject are correlated with each other. Integration focuses on making connections with real life. The activities and subjects should not be put in after tight compartments but these should be inter-related and integrated so as to develop the whole child.

6) Principle for future look or future orientation:
Curriculum must include those topics, content and learning experience that can help students to leading their future life.

7) Principle of flexibility:
At present time rapid developments are taking place in various fields. The content of curriculum cannot be same for all times. It must be dynamic and change with the changing times and should reflect the latest trends in

the field of education and psychology.

8) Principle of development Cultureand civilisation (Conservative):

The main function of education is to be preserve and transmit our heritage culture. This is important for human progress. Culture consists of traditions, customs, attitudes, skills, conduct, value and knowledge. Curriculum must include the traditions customs, values, moral etc. of the nation, so that it can be conserved.

9) Principle of creativity:

Creativity is the ability or capacity of a person to discover and explore new areas to create or produce a new idea, theory or object including the rearrangement or reshaping of what already exist. Educational institutions play a vital role in enhancing creative skills of individuals.

Through creativity, people become job creators rather then job seekers. Therefore, creativity should be encouraged among learners in school. Raymont say's "in curriculum that is suited to the needs of today and of the future there must be definitely creative subjects".

10) Principle of learnability:

The content should be what the students can learn and should be within their experience. Teachers should apply the theories on psychology of learning in order to present and sequence the content in such a way, to maximize the learning capacity of the students.

11) Principle of balance:

The selected content must be well balanced in respect to various maxims of curriculum development, such as simple to complex, known to unknown, concrete to abstract etc.

Conclusion:

It can be concluded that curriculum provides young people with the wide and adaptable set of skills to prepare them for their future roles in the society. In designing and review of curriculum different stakeholders are involved.

References:

1. https://www.academia.edu/35434053/
    FOUNDATIONS_OF_CURRICULUM
2. https://www.preservearticles.com/education/the-main-principles-of-curriculum-construction-may-be-mentioned-as-under/18040
3. https://educarepk.com/elements-of-curriculum.html

4. Dr. Sujit Pal, Koyel Kundu, Sourovi Thakur, Prof (Dr) Mita Banerjee; 2018; "Knowledge and curriculum". Part- II : Aaheli Publishers; ISBN No. 81-89169-23-8; Page No. 92

5. https://www.yogiraj.co.in/meaning-concept-and-types-of-curriculum

CHAPTER III

Components of Curriculum

Dr. Abhishek Srivastava*Divine Tomar

• • •

Introduction

Understanding the Curriculum

An interactive system of instruction and learning with particular goals, contents, tactics, measurement and resources is referred to as a curriculum. The successful transfer and/or development of knowledge, skills, and attitudes is the desired outcome of curriculum. Students practice and acquire competency in subject and applied learning skills through a standards-based series of designed experiences. Curriculum serves as a primary guide for all educators in terms of what is required for effective teaching and learning, ensuring that all students have access to challenging academic experiences.

A curriculum's structure, organisation, and concerns are designed to improve student learning and facilitate instruction. To effectively support instruction and learning, curriculum must include the essential goals, techniques, materials, and assessments. Curriculum is a list of concepts that should be taught to pupils in order for them to satisfy subject standards. What is taught in a certain course or subject is referred to as the curriculum.

The lessons and academic content taught in a school or in a specific course or programme are referred to as curricula. The curriculum is sometimes defined in dictionaries as the courses taught by a school, though it is rarely used in schools in this broad sense.

Definitions

1. *The curriculum encompasses a variety of technical and non technical courses that are required to complete a specific degree.*
2. *The curriculum includes everything that takes place, and everything that does not take place, within the purview of the school.*
3. *A curriculum refers to an interactive system of instruction and learning with specific goals, contents, strategies, measurement, and resources. The desired outcome of curriculum is successful transfer and/or*

development of knowledge, skills, and attitudes.

Curriculum typically refers to the knowledge and skills that students are expected to learn, which includes the learning standards or learning objectives that they are expected to meet; the units and lessons that teachers teach; the assignments and projects that students are given; and the books, materials, videos, presentations, and readings used in a classroom. The exact learning requirements, lessons, assignments, and resources used to arrange and teach a particular course are referred to as a teacher's curriculum. It's crucial to emphasize that, while curriculum can refer to a wide range of educational and instructional methods, educators frequently use the term in a very specific, technical sense. Most teachers devote a significant amount of time to thinking about, studying, discussing, and analysing curriculum, and many have developed a specialist's expertise in curriculum development—that is, they understand how to structure, organize, and deliver lessons in ways that support or accelerate student learning.

Perhaps the only truly "indigenous" concept in education is curriculum. Curriculum, despite its pervasiveness, is frequently assumed or taken for granted as part of the doxic vocabulary of education. The curriculum is the most important aspect of any educational system. Education involves the transmission of knowledge, attitudes, and abilities from one generation to the next, but the curriculum "reflects the forms of information, thinking habits, and cultural practices that a society thinks essential enough to pass on to subsequent generations." As a result, teachers must be familiar with the curriculum.

This handbook will assist you in grasping the concept of curriculum. Everything that a learner willingly receives and assimilates in order to affect his future behaviour is included in the curriculum. The "interaction" of pupils with the teacher, knowledge, and environment is referred to as curriculum. The curriculum changes the learner's knowledge and experience, allowing him to better manage circumstances in his environment. The planned engagement of pupils with instructional content, materials, resources, and mechanisms for evaluating the attainment of educational objectives may be included in the curriculum.

Components of Curriculum

The curriculum plays an important role in an educational system. It is somehow a blueprint which leads the teacher and the learner to reach the desired objectives. As a result, authorities have to design it in such a way that it could lead the teacher and the learner meet the desired learning outcomes.

The four components of the curriculum are :

1. Curriculum Aims, Goals and Objectives
2. Curriculum Content or Subject Matter
3. Curriculum Experience
4. Curriculum Evaluation

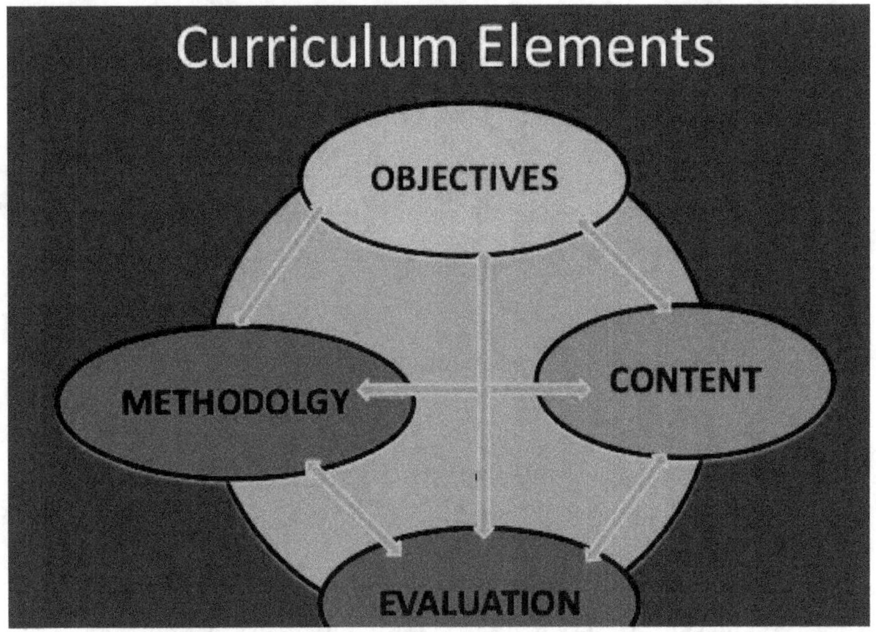

info4mystery.com

These four components of the curriculum are essential. These are interrelated to each other. Each of these has a connection to one another.

Aims, goals, and objectives can be simplified as "what is to be done", the subject matter/content: what subject matter is to be included, the learning experience" what instructional strategies, resources and activities will be employed, and the evaluation approaches , while curriculum evaluation is" what methods and instruments will be used to assess the results of the curriculum.

The curriculum aims, goals and objectives spell out what is to be done. It tries to capture what goals are to be achieved, the vision, the philosophy, the mission statement and objectives. Further, it clearly defines the purpose and what the curriculum is to be acted upon and try what to drive at.

In the same manner, curriculum has a content. In here, it contains information to be learned in school. It is an element or a medium through which the objectives are accomplished.

A primordial concern of formal education is primarily to transmit organized knowledge in distilled form to a new generation of young learners.

The traditional sources of what is taught and learned in school is precisely the foundation of knowledge, therefore, the sciences and humanities provide the basis of selecting the content of school learning.

In organizing the learning contents, balance, articulation, sequence, integration, and continuity form a sound content.

For the third component, the curriculum experience, instructional strategies and methods are the core of the curriculum. These instructional strategies and methods will put into action the goals and use of the content in order to produce an outcome.

These would convert the written curriculum to instruction. Moreover, mastery is the function of the teacher direction and student activity with the teacher supervision.

For the fourth component, the curriculum evaluation is an element of an effective curriculum. It identifies the quality, effectiveness of the program, process and product of the curriculum.

In summary, the components of a curriculum are distinct but interrelated to each other. These four components should be always present in a curriculum. I could say that these are essential ingredients to have an effective curriculum.

For example, in a curriculum, evaluation is also important so one could assess whether the objectives and aims have been meet or if not, he could employ another strategy which will really work out.

Curriculum experience could not be effective if the content is not clearly defined. The aims, goals and directions serve as the anchor of the learning journey, the content or subject matter serve as the meat of the educational journey, curriculum experience serves as the hands –on exposure to the real spectrum of learning and finally the curriculum evaluation serves as the barometer as to how far had the learners understood on the educational journey.

The four components of the curriculum are

Curriculum Aims, Goals and Objectives

What is to be done is spelled out in the curriculum's aims, goals, and objectives. It attempts to encapsulate the desired outcomes, as well as the vision, philosophy, mission statement, and objectives. The teaching objectives of any curriculum are usually determined at the start of the course. The language elements or skills that the students may learn during the programme should be explicitly stated in these objectives. Furthermore, it clearly outlines the goal and the curriculum to be followed, as well as what to aim for. The learning journey's ambitions, goals, and directions serve as its anchor. Designers who are aware of the significant problems they will face.

Everyone agrees that students should be able to gain information, skills, and attitudes through their education. Many people, however, desire the curricula to reflect the culture of the school and to promote the economic, political, social, and cultural interests of that society. At all levels, federal, state, and local, goals and objectives are determined based on philosophical, sociological, and psychological grounds. The content structure of the subject, the levels of pupils, and the type of test components are all taken into account when determining teaching and learning objectives. These goals are explicit and defined in behavioural language so that learning structures and conditions can be developed.

The distinction between objectives and goals is not as simple as it may appear. It is due to the fact that there are numerous parties involved in a course of study, including students, teachers, institutions, ministries of education, and so forth. Typically, objectives are articulated in terms of expected outcomes. A high school science teacher, for example, might create a chronological list of subjects to cover in a high school biological science course: human functions, utilisation of plant and animal resources, evolution and development, and so on (Williams, 2011). This type of list indicates what the scientific teacher intends to teach, but not the predicted outcomes of the lesson.

The instructor can utilize the content outline to prepare and guide instruction, but it is insufficient for stating behavioural objectives. Behavioral objectives must be linked to content in order to be beneficial in teaching.

It attempts to encapsulate the desired outcomes, as well as the vision, philosophy, mission statement, and objectives.

Curriculum Content or Subject Matter

The content of the curriculum is important. It contains knowledge that should be learnt in school. It is a component or a channel through which the goals are achieved. The transmission of organised knowledge in distilled form to a new generation of young learners is a primary concern of formal education. The substance of the educational journey is the substance or subject matter.

The sciences and humanities provide the ground for selecting the content of school learning because traditional sources of what is taught and acquired in school are precisely the foundation of knowledge.

Balance, articulation, sequence, integration, and continuity make a sound content when organising learning contents. It states precisely what the goal is and how the curriculum will be implemented, as well as what to aim for. Curriculum, like everything else, has a framework. It contains information on all of the subjects that must be learnt in school. It is a component or a channel through which the goals are achieved. The transmission of organised knowledge in distilled form to a new generation of young learners is a primary concern of formal education. Balance, articulation, sequence, integration, and continuity make a sound content when organising learning contents. Any subject's content is usually broad. It is broken down into sub-content and then into its constituent parts. These components are organised in a logical order. With the help of these content elements, behavioural objectives are defined. It's also known as teaching logic.

Curriculum Learning Experiences

The core of the curriculum is the curricular experience, teaching methodologies, and methodologies. Curriculum experience provides hands-on exposure to the whole range of learning possibilities. Curriculum experiences, the core and heart of the curriculum, will be linked to instructional strategies and approaches. These instructional strategies and approaches will put the goals and usage of the content into action in order to achieve a desired result. The published curriculum would be converted into instruction using these. Furthermore, mastery is a function of instructor guidance and student action under the supervision of the teacher. If the material is not clearly specified, the curriculum experience may be ineffective.

Curriculum experience refers to the teaching-learning methodologies, materials, and activities that will be used.

With the support of an effective teaching strategy, particular educational objectives can be met.

These instructional strategies and approaches will put the content's aims and uses into action to achieve a result. The published curriculum would be converted into instruction using these.

The behavioural objectives provide awareness and insight into the unique learning circumstances. The method is used to provide learning opportunities and encourage desired behavioural changes.

Furthermore, mastery is a function of instructor guidance and student action under the supervision of the teacher. Students must have the opportunity to practise the desired behaviour during the learning process. If the goal is to improve problem-solving skills, pupils should be given plenty of opportunities to do so. Students must be satisfied with their learning experience. Students require pleasurable experiences in order to establish and retain an interest in learning; unpleasurable experiences obstruct their learning. The learning experience must be tailored to the requirements and abilities of the pupils.

This implies that the teacher should start where the learner is at in terms of competence, and that existing information is the foundation for new knowledge. The same goal can be achieved through multiple learning experiences. The same idea can be learned in a variety of ways. A diverse set of experiences is more helpful for learning than a narrow set of experiences. Several learning objectives should be met during the learning experience.

Curriculum Evaluation

Curriculum evaluation is an important component of a well-designed curriculum. It determines the program's quality, effectiveness, and procedure as well as the curriculum's product. In a curriculum, evaluation is also crucial so that one may determine whether the objectives and goals have been met, and if not, if another technique will work better. The curriculum review serves as a yardstick for how far the students had progressed in their educational journey. All courses must include an aspect of evaluation in order to be effective. The official determination of the quality, efficacy, or usefulness of the curriculum's programme, methodology, and product is referred to as curriculum evaluation.

Several evaluation methods were suggested. Stufflebeam's CIPP Model is the most extensively utilized. The CIPP model's process is ongoing and crucial to the curriculum.

Curriculum evaluation is a component of an effective curriculum for the fourth element.

The term "curriculum evaluation" refers to the methodologies and tools that will be used to examine the curriculum's outcomes. It determines the program's quality, effectiveness, and procedure as well as the curriculum's product. A criteria-referenced test is used to assess a student's level of achievement. It displays the efficiency of the strategy of teaching and other components.

The feedback provided through evaluation interpretation is used to improve the programme and its components.

A curriculum review is also necessary in order to determine whether the objectives and goals have been met, and if not, to devise a new method that will be effective. Curriculum evaluation is a scientific foundation for 'curriculum development.'

References

- https://en.m.wikipedia.org/wiki/Curriculum
- http://www1.udel.edu/educ/whitson/897s05/files/definitions_
- of_curriculum.htm#:~:text=Curriculum%20is%20the%20outline%20of,
- strategies%2C%20measurement%2C%20and%20resources.
- http://www.meshguides.org/guides/node/1527
- https://www.edglossary.org/curriculum/
- http://olga-syscurriculum.blogspot.com/2011/05/4-components-of-curriculum-cayadong.html?m=1
- https://www.slideshare.net/adirepse15/components-of-curriculum-51575713
- https://www.doe.mass.edu/acls/frameworks/components.html

- https://www.scribd.com/presentation/421832597/Components-of-Curriculum-Design

CHAPTER IV

Curriculum: Foundation, Evaluation Goals and Methodologies

**Muskan Gupta

• • •

Introduction

Curriculum studies (CS) is a subfield of curriculum and instruction that focuses on understanding curricula as a driving factor in human learning. Curriculum Studies is a curriculum that teaches students how to use successful instructional methods and how to be professional teachers at all levels of education. It is used in curriculum and education to apply theoretical foundations. Students gain knowledge, skills, and attitudes about how to conduct research, create, develop, implement, evaluate, and disseminate innovative educational techniques in a variety of learning situations. Everything that occurs in the classroom, including extracurricular activities, supervision, and interpersonal connections, is referred to as curriculum. The curriculum is what the school instructs students to learn both inside and outside of the classroom. Everything organised by school employees is referred to as curriculum. Learners go through a sequence of experiences in school that make up their curriculum. A learner's curriculum is what he or she encounters as a result of their education.

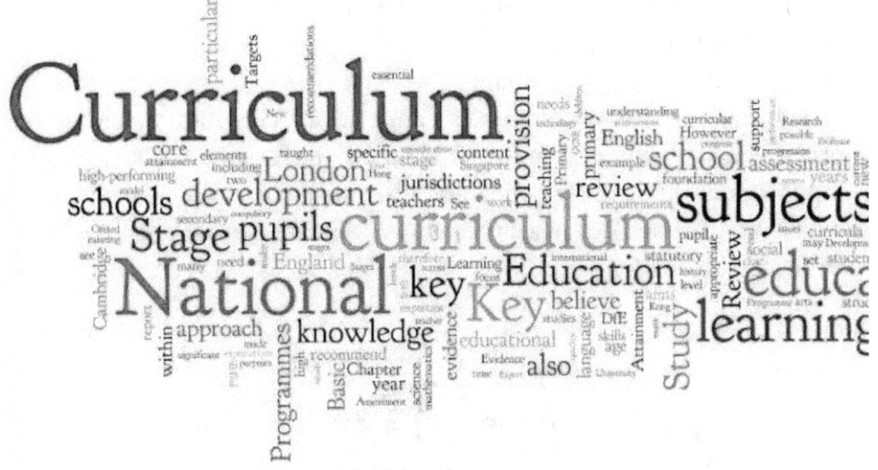

thekingstonacademy.org

If you look at curricular definitions, you'll see that they fall into five categories:

1. Curriculum as a service or a product: - a programmer, a document, a piece of electronic media, or a piece of multimedia.

2. Curriculum as desired learnings: - normally, programs are given, as well as curricular sequences of study in standards that serve as benchmarks and gateways.

3. Curriculum as desired learnings: - objectives, substance, concepts, generalizations, and results.

4. Curriculum as a learner's perspective: - planned and unanticipated actions.

5. Curriculum that isn't visible: - is it feasible to find out what pupils learn that isn't intended - unless users prepare for it - or is it even conceivable?

Components of Curriculum

The curriculum is crucial in every educational institution. It's a kind of road map that guides the instructor and the student toward the targeted outcomes. As a result, authorities must build it in such a manner that it can help both the instructor and the student achieve the targeted learning results.

The curriculum consists of four components:

1. Curriculum Goals, Objectives, and Aims
2. The content of the curriculum, or the subject matter
3. Experiential Curriculum
4. Evaluation of the Curriculum

These four curricular components are critical. These are linked to one another. Each of these things is linked to the others. A curriculum's components are unique, but they are all connected. These four elements should always be included in a curriculum. These are necessary components for a successful curriculum.

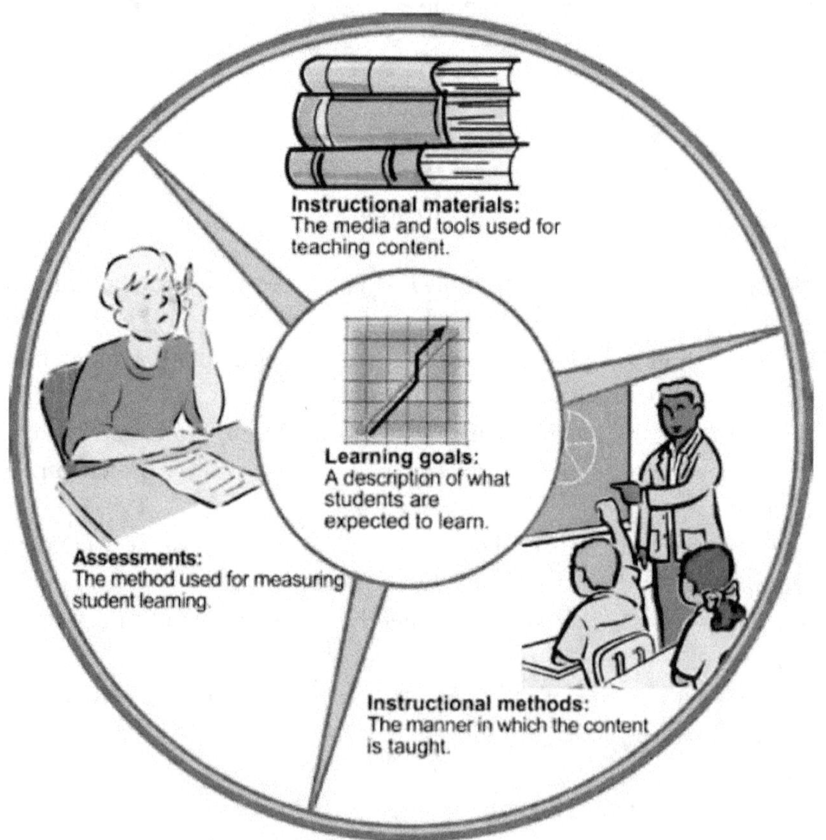

Enter Captioniris.peabody.vanderbilt.edu

For example, in a curriculum, assessment is critical so that one may determine whether the objectives and goals have been met, and if not, implement a different technique that will really work.

If the material is not clearly specified, the curriculum experience may be ineffective. The learning journey's aims, goals, and directions serve as the anchor, the content or subject matter serves as the meat, curriculum experience serves as hands-on exposure to the real spectrum of learning, and curriculum evaluation serves as the barometer for how far the learners understood on the educational journey.

Curriculum Evaluation

Curriculum evaluation is an important part of the development process. A faculty member can determine if a curriculum is meeting its objectives and whether students are learning. Evaluation is primarily the dissemination of data in order to aid decision-making at various levels of curriculum development. This information might apply to the entire programmer or just a few of its components. Selection of criteria, data gathering, and analysis are all part of the evaluation process. It entails gathering data in order to assess the value of a programmer or technique. It is a broad phrase that encompasses all methods of determining construction results and goes beyond standardized examinations.

Curriculum evaluation is a necessary and fundamental aspect of the entire curriculum development process. It is not a "tail-end-process," but rather a continuous activity. Evaluation and planning are two activities that happen virtually concurrently and in real time. Planning is based on assessment, and evaluation is based on planning. As a distinct state, though, evaluation has its own entity.

Curriculum evaluation goals include:

1. Determining a program's outcomes.

2. To assist in the decision of whether or not to approve or reject a programme.

3. Determine whether or not the course content needs to be revised.

4. Assist in the future creation of curricular materials in order to ensure ongoing improvement.

5. Improving teaching methods and instructional strategies.

Evaluation Methodologies for Curriculum:

1. Formative evaluation: It takes place throughout the construction of a curriculum. Its goal is to help with the educational program's improvement. During the development phase, a program's merits are assessed. The assessment findings provide programmers information and allow them to fix any issues they find.

2. Summative Assessment: In summative evaluation, a curriculum's ultimate impacts are assessed against its stated goals. It occurs following the completion and implementation of the programme.

3. Diagnostic evaluation: Diagnostic evaluation has two purposes: it may be used to appropriately position students at the start of an educational level (such as secondary school), or it can be used to find the underlying reason of student learning deviations in any field of study.

Foundation of Curriculum

Curriculum foundations are the philosophical, psychological, social, and historical understandings that are used to evaluate educational systems and policies.

The foundations of curriculum establish what constitutes appropriate sources from which to generate the field's theories, concepts, and ideas, as well as the exterior bounds of curricular knowledge. Philosophical, psychological, social, and historical aspects are the universally acknowledged foundations of curriculum, as indicated below:

educarepk.com

Philosophical foundation of curriculum

Curriculum decisions are based on a variety of factors, many of which are related to education. These concerns include the aim of learning, subject matter sources, the nature of the teaching/learning process, and learner characteristics. These choices are founded on or grounded in some core principles that stem from one's educational philosophy. This is what allowed philosophy to be considered or accepted as one of the curriculum's pillars. Idealism, Realism, Existentialism, Pragmatism, Essentialism, Perennialism, and Deconstructionism are some of the philosophical ideas that impact curriculum.

Philosophy assists us in managing our own personal system of beliefs and values, i.e., how we see the world around us and how we define what is essential to us. Because philosophical questions have always had an impact on society and educational institutions, studying and comprehending educational philosophy in connection to curriculum creation is essential.

Essentially, educational philosophy influences and, to a greater extent, decides our educational selections and options. This is because persons in charge of curricular decisions must be clear about their own beliefs or belief systems. This is due to the fact that imprecise or muddled views will inevitably lead to a muddled and perplexing curriculum.

Psychological foundation of curriculum

Educational psychology is a branch of psychology that studies how individuals learn. Psychologists are interested in identifying patterns in human behavior in order to better understand and predict behavior. Educational psychology develops teaching and learning ideas that impact teacher-student behavior within the setting of the curriculum. This is due to psychology's role as a unifying factor in the learning process. For example, renowned educator John Dewey recognizes that psychology is the study of how an individual learner interacts with things and people in his or her environment. The amount and kind of learning is determined by the quality of this contact.

Psychology in general, and educational psychology in particular, aids in curriculum decision-making by assisting in the selection and arrangement of suitable objectives, learning experiences, and evaluation techniques, as well as judgments about the curriculum's breadth. Many curricular decisions are influenced by psychology. The best way to understand the psychological effects of curriculum is to look at learning theories. Behavioral learning theories, cognitive and developmental learning theories, and humanistic learning theories are the three basic types of learning theories.

Social foundation of curriculum

Schools are an integral element of society and exist to serve it. The curriculum of a society has an impact on that society. Schools may form and mold society through their curriculum teaching, while society can influence the curriculum. Rarely is a curriculum established that does not reflect society. To comprehend how the substance of education is shaped in every culture, we must first comprehend the link between education and other social institutions. To put it another way, we need to look at the social factors that form the curriculum to understand what is taught, how it is taught, and why it is taught.

Knowing the social underpinnings of curriculum is essential for deciding what should be included in the curriculum and, ultimately, what happens in the classroom. A curriculum should be capable of preparing pupils for both now and the future. To put it another way, a curriculum should adjust to local, national, and global social situations in order to meet the wants and needs of students.

Historical foundation of curriculum

History is the product of human activity involving participation in various events. To be confident of what will happen in the future, one must look back at what has already happened. As a result, the curriculum's historical base tackles many stages of human growth. Students are aware that cultural events and personal difficulties occur on a regular basis. We frequently don't know how to make sense of what's going on since the amount of events and concerns we're dealing with is so overwhelming.

History may assist students develop a better understanding of current events and concerns. The ability to deconstruct and examine experiences is a crucial component of critical thinking. As a result of the historical basis of the curriculum, a study of politics, economics, geography, agriculture, religion, and sociocultural activities is expounded in order to be confident with the past and predict the future for the society's well-being. When developing curriculum, curriculum planners usually make sure that the historical viewpoint is effectively portrayed in order to capture not only the local flavor but also worldwide historical perspectives.

Principles of Curriculum Construction in India

1. Child-centeredness principle:

The modern approach to curriculum development should be paedocentric and democratic, in the sense that the child should be at the center of the teaching-learning process and should actively participate in it. The kid should be at the center of all curricular activities. At the time of curriculum development, his abilities, interests, attitudes, and needs should all be taken into account.

2. The Flexibility and Variety Principle:

The Secondary Education Commission (1953) proposed that secondary school curricula give diversity and flexibility. Modern curricula should be built in accordance with local and individual demands and circumstances. In order to meet the demands of each individual, the curriculum must be varied. Learners should have the option of choosing their own subjects. Learners should not be pressured into enrolling in a programme of study. Individual variations between pupils must be taken into consideration.

3. Correlation Principle:

Various subjects in the curriculum should be effectively coordinated, and every subject should have some relationship with other subjects that instructors and students should be aware of.

4. Integration Principle:

The integration principle is critical for the development of a child's overall personality. Various courses included in the curriculum at a given level of school, such as history, civics, geography, and social studies, should be integrated. The integration concept should be used to organize various operations.

5. Community Service Principle:

The current curriculum should be linked to everyday living in the community. The nature and substance of curriculum should be determined by the community's requirements and conditions. The curriculum should be structured in such a way that it allows for the most efficient use of community resources for educational growth and vice versa.

6. Values Principle:

A variety of desired ideals must be instilled in our children in the growing society. As a result, modern curricula should include provisions for instilling social, moral, spiritual, democratic, and artistic ideals.

7. The Totality Principle:

The Secondary Education Commission has also emphasized this notion, stating that a whole range of learning experiences must be provided to students in the classroom, as well as in the library, laboratory, workshop, and playground, as well as via casual interactions between instructors. In this sense, the school's entire life becomes a curriculum that may impact students' lives at any time.

Recommendations and Findings

1. The University and each college should be encouraged to include the objective of educating students for citizenship in a technologically and information-rich society in their mission statements. Students must be able to access, utilize, and analyze information that is relevant to their vocations and lives as citizens, as well as communicate and collaborate successfully utilizing current technology tools.

2. Each college's curriculum committees should determine the information and technology capabilities students should have to accomplish the college's goal, with some support from the University. The committees should also make sure that the curriculum is organized to assist students fulfil the needed competences in each circumstance. Rationale: Students must be prepared to utilize technology, according to new statewide K-12 requirements. We should build on and exceed these norms as a public university. Competencies might be established on a college-wide or major-by-major basis. Model competencies should be developed by a university-wide advisory council as a reference, but schools should be allowed to design their own competency criteria. These might include ways for undergraduate and graduate students to get an information technology certificate, as well as other options.

3. Individual schools should engage in strategic planning procedures for the continued integration and management of technology in the education they provide, which should include wide participation from the campus community. Rationale: Taking a broad (and long) view is the best approach to define both the role of instructional technology in a college's curriculum and the necessity for faculty development and training activities, in addition to ensuring students have chances to study and apply technology in their coursework.

4. In order to coordinate work with instructional technology and encourage cross-campus efforts, the University should engage in strategic planning/management as an ongoing process with wide representation from the University community. Rationale: University-wide planning is crucial to creating efficiency in coordinating support and synergies in projects that span campuses, which is a benefit of a multi-campus system.

Conclusion

Finally, in today's heterogeneous culture, the curriculum should be inclusive in order to promote equality and diversity. The teacher has a crucial role in curriculum development, implementation, and evaluation. It should aim to make learning more meaningful and pleasant for students, as well as to encourage them to be more creative and self-reliant. It should also allow them to put what they've learned into practice. It seems to be one thing to create an excellent curriculum. The achievement of not only the level, general, and specialized objectives, but more crucially the national aims and values, requires proper interpretation and implementation. Effective curriculum implementation supervision aids the end consumer, the learner, in becoming the greatest possible output. Assume the role of curricular supervisors.

Bibliography

- Cain, D. (2017). *"KENYA INSTITUTE OF CURRICULUM DEVELOPMENT"*. Retrieved from SlidePlayer: https://slideplayer.com/slide/10570872/
- Department of Educational Management, P. a. (2021). *CURRICULUM STUDIES*. Retrieved from https://eap.uonbi.ac.ke/schools/curriculum-studies
- DiFlorio, P. D. (2016). *Curriculum evaluation.* Retrieved from https://pubmed.ncbi.nlm.nih.gov/2601681/
- Dr. Olga C. Alonsabe, C. L. (2012). *Systems of Developing, Implementing and Assessing Curriculum.* Retrieved from http://olga-syscurriculum.blogspot.com
- GULZAR, A. A. (n.d.). *Foundations of Curriculum.* Retrieved from Educare: https://educarepk.com/foundations-of-curriculum.
- Iyer, N. (n.d.). *Curriculum Construction in India | Education.* Retrieved from https://www.yourarticlelibrary.com/education/curriculum-construction-in-india-education/84842
- Nguyen, T. L. (2019). *My Opinion about Curriculum Redesign in the 21st Century.* Retrieved from https://medium.com/age-of-awareness/my-opinion-about-curriculum-redesign-in-the-21st-century-2f11f855d0cd
- Notes, S. L. (2022). *Curriculum Evaluation Meaning, Importance & Objective.* Retrieved from Study Lecture Notes: http://studylecturenotes.com/curriculum-evaluation-meaning-importance-objective/
- *Page 3: Curricular Components.* (2021). Retrieved from IRIS Center : https://iris.peabody.vanderbilt.edu/module/udl/cresource/q2/p03/

- *RECOMMENDATIONS RE FACULTY AND CURRICULUM DEVELOPMENT SETTING AND ACHIEVING GOALS*. (n.d.). Retrieved from https://studylib.net/doc/18000705/recommendations-re-faculty-and-curriculum-development--se
- Sweetland's, D. R. (n.d.). *Introduction to Curriculum: It's Development and General Classification of Different Definitions*. Retrieved from https://www.homeofbob.com/pedagogy/plan/curDev/defIntro.htm
- Wikipedia. (2021). *Curriculum studies*. Retrieved from https://en.wikipedia.org/wiki/Curriculum_studies.

CHAPTER V

Concept, Types, Stages, and Reform of Curriculum

****Dr. Suprasad Lodh**

• • •

Introduction:

- The term curriculum has been derived from a Latin word 'Currere' which means a 'race course' or a runway on which one runs to reach a goal. If the teacher is the guide, the curriculum is the path. Curriculum is the total structure of ideas and activities.

The curriculum places an important role in an educational system or we can say curriculum is the heart of education process. It is somehow a blueprint which leads the teacher and the learner to reach the desired objectives. As a result, authorities have to design it so that it could lead the teacher and the learner to meet the desired learning outcomes. Though the child's development and growth is the main consideration of curriculum construction yet his social behaviour is also to be suitably developed, both the individual development and the social development of the child deserve equal attention.

Meaning of Curriculum:

Curriculum is an important part of education. The term Curriculum has been derived from a Latin would "Currere" which means a 'race course' or a runway on which one runs to reach a goal. The term Curriculum refers to the lessons and academic content taught in a school or in a specific course or program.

It is curriculum through which the general aims of a school education receive Concrete expression. Curriculum is the total sum of all the activities and experiences provided by the institution to the learners for their all-around development and for achieving the goals of education.

Curriculum is a tool in the hands of artist (the teacher) to make his materials (the pupils) according to his ideal (objective) in his studio (the institution). Curriculum is not just written on page, but the curriculum is reflected in teachers'behaviour& conduct. Everything done in the institution to Curriculum like classroom instructions, students Activities, work experiences, school parties etc. Therefore, we can say - Curriculum in theheart of education process.

Concept of Curriculum:

The literal meaning of curriculum is derived from a Latin word 'currere' the source of this was another Latin word 'Currer' that means a chariot race runway or path I,e laid to reach the goal. From that sence of of meaning the primary meaning of curriculum is race course or runway or pre planned way of an educational system. In education curriculum is used in two concepts-

a. Traditional Concept

a. Modern concept

Components of Curriculum:

Curriculum plays an important role in an educational system. There are 4 basic components of curriculum and these are ----

a. Curriculum objectives.
b. Curriculum content or subject matter.
c. Curriculum experience.
d. Curriculum evaluation.

These four components of the curriculum are essential. These are interrelated to each other. Each of these has a connection to one another. I could say that these are essential ingredients to have an effective Curriculum.

a. **Curriculum objectives:**

The Curriculum aims, goals and objectives spell-out what is to be done. It tries to capture what goals are to be achieved, the vision, the philosophy, the mission statement and objectives. Further, it clearly defines the purpose and what the curriculum is to be acted upon and try what to drive at.

There are four main factors affecting the formulation of curriculum objectives. These are—

i.   The society.
ii. The knowledge.
iii. The learner.
iv. The learningprocesses.

All of these factors are to be considered while selecting and formulating the curriculum objectives.

b. Curriculum content or subject matter:

A second element is the content of the curriculum. It contains information to be learned in school. It is an element or a medium through which the objectives are accomplished.

One of the important considerationsis the selection of content for a subject. At the time of subject matter selection, the following factors are to be kept in mind:

a. Available sources and resources.
b. Demand of society
c. International needs.
d. Level and age of the learner or the student.
e. Methods of content organization.
f. Number of courses offered.
g. Scope of subject matter.
h. System of examination.
a. Quantity and qualification of teaching staff.

c. Learning experiences (methods of delivering knowledge):

The term "learning experiences" is not the same as the content with which course deals nor the activities performed by the teacher. The term "learning experience" refers to the interaction between the learner and the external condition in the environment to which he/she can react. Learning takes place through the active behaviour of the student.

d. Curriculum evaluation:

Curriculum evaluation is different from a student evaluation. It is a broader term being used to make a judgement about the worth and effectiveness of curriculum. Curriculum evaluation is also important in a sense that one could assess whether the aim and objectives have been met or not.

Foundation of curriculum:

Just as curriculum can be defined in a variety of ways, one can approach the evaluation and creation of curriculum through more than one foundational lens:

Philosophical, sociological and psychological. All three of this hold importance in influencing curriculum and instruction.

Philosophical Foundations: Philosophy lays the strong foundation of any curriculum. A curriculum planner or specialist, implementer or the teacher, school heads, evaluator anchors his/her decision-making process on a sound philosophy. Philosophy provides educators, teachers and curriculum makers with framework for planning, implementing and evaluating curriculum in school, answering what schools are for, what subjects are important, how students should learn and what materials and methods should be used. In decision-making, philosophy provides the starting point and will be used for the succeeding decision-making.

The following four educational philosophies relate to curriculum:

- **Perennialism:** The focus in the curriculum is classical subjects, literary analysis and considers the curriculum as constant.
- **Essentialism:** The essential skills of the 3 R's and essential subjects of English, Science, History, Math and Foreign Language is the focus of the curriculum.
- **Progressivism:** The curriculum is focused on students' interest, human problems and affairs. The subjects are interdisciplinary, integrative and interactive.
- **Reconstructionism:** The focus of the curriculum is on present and future trends and issues of national and international interests.

Psychological Foundations: Curriculum is influenced by psychology. Psychology provides information about the teaching and learning process. It also seeks answers as to how a curriculum be organized in order to achieve students' learning at the optimum level, and as to what amount of information they can absorb in learning the various contents of the curriculum. Psychology provides basis for the teaching and learning process. It unifies elements of the learning process and some of the sum of questions which can be addressed by psychological foundation.

Types of Curriculum:

From applications point of view in education curriculum mainly classified in two ways-

- Hidden Curriculum
- Written Curriculum

Some important classifications of written curriculum those are used in different educational institution are-

1. Subject centered curriculum
2. Activity centered curriculum
3. Experience centered curriculum
4. Core curriculum
5. Integrated curriculum
6. Learner/ Student-centered curriculum

Stages of specific curriculum:

- Pre-primary curriculum
- Primary curriculum
- Secondary curriculum
- Higher Secondary curriculum

Curriculum reforms in India – National curriculum frame work:
Curriculum reforms in India 9NCF 2000 – 2005)

1. Context and Concern
2. Organization of curriculum of Elementary and Secondary stage
3. Organization curriculum of Higher Secondary stage
4. Evaluation

Principles of curriculum construction:
Curriculum is based on following important principles: -

1) principals of utility:

Curriculum should be useful rather than decorative. The curriculum must have practical utility for students.

2) Principle of child Centeredness:

Curriculum should be child- centred. It should be based on the child's needs, interests, abilities, aptitude age level and circumstances.

Infact, curriculum is meant to bring about the development of the child in the desired direction so that he is able to adjust well in life.

3) Principle of community centeredness:

According to the curriculum growth and development of child is very important but his social behaviour is also to be suitably developed. He should understand member of the community and try to solve them in a systematic way as he is to live in and for the society. So, the values, attitudes and skills that are prevailing in the community must be reflected in curriculum.

4) Principles of activity centeredness:

Curriculum must be full of activities. As child learn maximum things from activities. It should be connected with the child's desires and needs. The useful activities both in the class room and outside the class room should be provided.

5) Principles of interrelation of subject:

Curriculum should be such that all the subject are correlated with each other. Integration focuses on making connections with real life. The activities and subjects should not be put in after tight compartments but these should be inter-related and integrated so as to develop the whole child.

6) Principle for future look or future orientation:

Curriculum must include those topics, content and learning experience that can help students to leading their future life.

7) Principle of flexibility:

At present time rapid developments are taking place in various fields. The content of curriculum cannot be same for all times. It must be dynamic and change with the changing times and should reflect the latest trends in the field of education and psychology.

8) Principle of development Culture and Civilisation (Conservative):

The main function of education is to be preserve and transmit our heritage culture. This is important for human progress. Culture consists of traditions, customs, attitudes, skills, conduct, value and knowledge. Curriculum must include the traditions customs, values, moral etc. of the nation, so that it can be conserved.

9) Principle of creativity:

Creativity is the ability or capacity of a person to discover and explore new areas to create or produce a new idea, theory or object including the rearrangement or reshaping of what already exist. Educational institutions play a vital role in enhancing creative skills of individuals.

Through creativity, people become job creators rather then job seekers. Therefore, creativity should be encouraged among learners in school. Raymont say's "in curriculum that is suited to the needs of today and of the future there must be definitely creative subjects".

10) Principle of learnability:

The content should be what the students can learn and should be within their experience. Teachers should apply the theories on psychology of learning in order to present and sequence the content in such a way, to maximize the learning capacity of the students.

11) Principle of balance:

The selected content must be well balanced in respect to various maxims of curriculum development, such as simple to complex, known to unknown, concrete to abstract etc.

Conclusion

Curriculum is the crux of the whole educational process. Without curriculum, we cannot conceive any educational Endeavour. • The curriculum in a literal sense, a pathway towards a

goal. • Curriculum is actually what happens during a course i.e., lecture , demonstrations, field visits, the work with the client and so on. • Curriculum also means a written description of what happens.

▶ Curriculum is an important element of education. Aims of education are reflected in the curriculum. In other words, the curriculum is determined by the aims of life and society. Aims of life and society are subject to constant change.

Curriculum framers should used practical approach rather than ideological, reorganizing of recent curricula, solving language issue, facing controversies on curriculum change, obtaining continuous feedback and developing hearing in society at the same time. It is imperative for scholars to have effective communication skills and dynamic personality to incorporate the future trends without creating conflicts and confusion in the society. They need to know the skill to motivate and mould high ups for future changes and bring changes without development of controversies.

References

- Dr. Jayanta Mete, Parthita iswas, Pranay Pandey-"Knowledge and Curriculum'- Rita Book
- Agency.
- Dr. Kaushik Chakrabarti & Rekheebrita Biswas-Knowledge and Curriculum- Aahali Publishers.
- Dr. Sujit Pal, Kayal Kundu, Sourovi Thakur-"Knowledge and Curriculum"-Aahali
- Publishers.

CHAPTER VI

Stage Specific Curriculum

Mr. Uday Modak,*Mrs. Mala modak

• • •

Introduction:

These are nothing but the fundamental stages that every child has to go through while studying in the Indian education system. Yes, by definition, this is the aptest and concise explanation of what pre-primary, primary, and secondary education is. But each curriculum has different teaching methods and styles.

Each child starts from the pre-primary stage and ends his or her high school education by completing and passing the higher secondary board as per the authorities' grading system. If we go by the book, this is it, and there is nothing more to discuss or say about it. But if we go by concern and curiosity to understand what these stages are, how they are different from each other, and how they shape each student for the better part of their lives.

If we go by explaining it in one line, all that the curriculum of these stages does is that, in pre-primary, you learn how to speak, how to write. In the primary, you learn what to write and what to speak, and in the secondary stage, you are made sure to be able to write and speak well-informed and relevant information for the rest of your lives. The Pre-primary is also called the Kindergarten in India; the term was first introduced by Mr. Friedrich Frobel in 1837, which literally means children's garden.

After high school, the higher secondary stage is considered to be the last phase of schooling, and after that, the students attend college most commonly in the stream they choose after 10th standard.

Objectives of the Study:

1. The study will discuss about the stage Specific Curriculum.

2. The study wills emphasis the different stage of Education.

Stage Specific Curriculum:

A state-specific course means that we have created a course based on one specific set of standards for one state. The Edmonton Curriculum team creates state-specific courses using our standard course-development process of research, design, creation (writing, editing, and production), and publishing. Let's take a closer look at what this means for a state-specific course.

Education in India follows a uniform structure of school education which is known as the 10+2 system. This system is being followed by all Indian States and Union Territories. But not all of them follow a distinct pattern as per the system.

1. Pre Primary Stage –

Pre-primary education in India is provided to children between 3–6 years by Kindergarten, Play way or Play Schools. These schools have varying terminology for different levels of classes, beginning from – Pre-Nursery, Nursery, KG, LKG (Lower Kindergarten) and UKG (Upper Kindergarten). Most of the pre-primary education in India is provided by private schools.

2. The Primary Stage –

Primary Education in India offered by both private and government schools usually consist of students aged between 5 to 12 years. The duration of study in this stage is 4-5 years. Common subjects include English, Hindi, Mathematics, Environmental Science and General Knowledge. Sometimes also termed as Elementary Education, it is free in government schools but it is paid in the private schools. The Government has made elementary education compulsory for children between the age group of years 6 and 14. Most of the primary education provided by primary schools in India is imparted from class 1st to class 4th or 5th. Some of the states/UTs which follow 1st to 5th class of primary education are Andhra Pradesh, Arunachal Pradesh, Bihar, Haryana, Himachal Pradesh, Jammu & Kashmir, Madhya Pradesh, Manipur, Orissa, Punjab, Chandigarh, Delhi, Karaikal and Yanam regions of Pondicherry etc. Some of the states/UTs which follow 1st to 4th classes of primary education are Assam, Goa, Gujarat, Karnataka, Kerala, Maharashtra, Meghalaya, Mizoram, Nagaland, Dadra & Nagar Haveli, Daman & Diu, Lakshadweep and Mahe region of Pondicherry.

3. The Secondary Stage –

Secondary Stage of education covering 2-3 years of academic study starts with classes 8th-10th. consisting of students aged between 14-16 years. The schools which impart education up till 10th class are known as Secondary Schools, High Schools, Senior Schools etc. Some of the states/UTs which follow 8th-10th class of secondary stage are Goa, Gujarat, Karnataka, Kerala,

Dadra & Nagar Haveli, Daman & Diu, Lakshadweep etc. Some of the states/ UTs which follow 9th -10th class of secondary stage are Punjab, Rajasthan, Sikkim, Tamil Nadu, Andaman & Nicobar Islands, Chandigarh, Delhi, Karaikal region of Pondicherry etc.

4. Higher Secondary Stage –

Senior Secondary Education in India is of only 2 years. There is uniformity on this level of education in terms of duration and classes i.e. all the States/UTs follow this 10+2 pattern. Senior Secondary Schools in India include classes 11th to 12th. consisting students aged between 16-18 years. At this level of education students have the freedom to choose their preferred stream and subjects. They can pursue Arts, Commerce, Science (medical & non medical). The schools which provide education up till 12th class are commonly known as Senior Secondary Schools or Higher Secondary Schools. Some universities and colleges also offer the education of these classes.

Different stages of education:

a) Lower Primary Stage:

(Classes I-IV)- The child should receive instruction in the basic tools of learning such as reading, writing and computation and should learn to adjust to his surrounding through an elementary study of his physical and social environment.

For a sound foundation of mother-tongue, no language other than this should be introduced during the first four years. The curriculum should be gradually expanded and developed in keeping with the child's growth and development.The curriculum at this stage should include:

(i) One language, the mother-tongue or the regional language,

(ii) Arithmetic,

(iii) Study of the environment (covering Science and Social Studies in classes III and IV)

(iv) Creative activities.

(v) Work-experience and Social Service

(vi) Health education

b) Higher Primary Stage:

Classes V-VII) The study of second language will be added to mother-tongue; arithmetic skill will be used in acquisition of more difficult mathematical knowledge; environmental activities will lead to the study of natural and physical sciences, history, geography and civics. The constructive and creative skills will provide the basis for the practice of simple arts and crafts. And the practice of healthy living will serve as foundation for physical education. At this stage the curriculum will cover the following:

(i) Two language; Mother-tongue and Hindi or English; it to be noted that a third language (English, Hindi or a regional language) may be introduced on an optional basis.

(ii) Mathematics,

(iii) General Science,

(iv) Social Studies (History, Geography and Civics)

(v) "Art,

(vi) Work Experience and Social Service,

(vii) Physical Education, and

viii) Education in Moral and Spiritual values.

(c) Secondary Stage:

The curriculum should meet the needs of the adolescent individuals as well as the democratic society in which the child is expected to participate as a citizen on reaching maturity. The secondary school curriculum should contain necessary educational elements for cultivation of certain skills, elements, attitudes, and qualities of character viz. capacity for clear thinking, the ability to communicate easily with his fellowmen, a sense of true patriotism and an appreciation of the value of productive work. The needs of adolescence are related not only to the acquisition of knowledge and the promotion of intellectual ability, but the fuller development of physical, emotional aesthetic and moral aspects of personality. Provision has, therefore, to be made in the curriculum for the programme of physical education. At this stage (classes VIII-X) the curriculum should include;

(i) Three languages: Mother-tongue, Hindi and English in non-Hindi area and in Hindi area mother-tongues (Hindi), English and one of the 15 modern Indian languages other than Hindi, it may here be noted the a classical language may be studied in addition to the above 3 languages on an optional basis.

(ii) Mathematics,

(iii) General Science,

(iv) History, Geography and Civics,

(v) Art,

(vi) Work-experience and Social Service,

(vii) Physical Education, and Education in moral and spiritual values.

(d) Subject Areas of Higher Secondary (+2) Course:

The existing one year higher-secondary course will soon cover a two-year period after the 10 years schooling pattern. The whole question of higher secondary curriculum will have to be carefully examined and details worked out by an expert body consisting of representatives of the Universities, State Board of School Education and State Department of Education. The curriculum will cover a large area than that of the 10 year pattern of curriculum as follows:

(i) Any two Indian languages including M.I.L. English and any classical language,

(ii) Any three subjects from among History, Geography, Economics, Logic, Psychology, Sociology, Art, Physics, Chemistry, Mathematics, Biology, Geology, Home Science and an additional language,

(iii) Work-experience and Social Service,

(iv) Physical Education,

(v) Art and Craft, and

(vi) Education on Moral and Spiritual value.

Conclusion:

Though there are undeniable loopholes in the Indian education system, all of that can be eliminated with continuous efforts. Also, one should focus not only on them but also on society as a member and work to bring the change we speak of so boldly.

Having said all this, we hope you understand the importance of pre-primary education, primary education, secondary, and higher secondary education. Also, how the Indian education system and curriculum works and operates at each school level with a different syllabus.

References:

- https://revivingindianeducation.wordpress.com/about/levels-or-stages-of-education-in-india-today/
- https://blog.edmentum.com/edmentum%E2%80%99s-commitment-state-specific-courses
- https://www.preservearticles.com/education/curriculum-at-different-stages/4861
- https://www.orchidsinternationalschool.com/blog/child-learning/understanding-curriculum/
- https://www.yourarticlelibrary.com/education/three-stages-of-education-primary-middle-and-lower-secondary/44874

CHAPTER VII

Curriculum:Transaction and Evaluation

Dr. Ekata Gupta,*Pranati Das

• • •

Introduction

Curriculum Transaction is the successful and desirable execution of curriculum contents based on the curriculum's stated goals and objectives. Curriculum Transaction entails excellent planning for providing learning experiences for its learners, as well as the organization of planning, administration/implementation of the organized planning, and evaluation of the implementations by the implementer and experts in the field.

Curriculum transaction, sometimes known as curriculum management, is the process of creating and organizing a certain subject area's curriculum for various levels of education, as well as regularly monitoring it as it is implemented.

Components

Curriculum Transaction is defined as the process of planning curriculum for various levels of study in a subject area and regularly monitoring its execution. Curriculum Transaction is the successful and desirable execution of curriculum contents based on the curriculum's stated goals and objectives.

The Curriculum Transaction entails:

- Effective planning for providing learners with learning opportunities,
- Planning organization
- Organizational planning administration/implementation
- The implementer and specialists in the relevant field evaluate the implementations.

The following are some of the conditions for a successful curriculum transaction:

- Planning
- Clarity in thinking

- Knowing how we'll do business
- Examining the work
- Teamwork is essential.
- Communication clarity
- addressing children at various levels
- interacting with children on a variety of levels
- Organize your time
- Alertness
- Material management
- Setup of the room
- The manner in which we communicate with youngsters

Methods of Curriculum Evaluation

Curriculum evaluation incorporates dozens of diverse definitions, techniques, and methods from two independent and complex fields: curriculum and evaluation. As a result, curriculum evaluation cannot be straightforward or uniform.

The diversity of evaluation typologies, models, concepts, and procedures suggests a shift from a monolithic to a pluralist conceptualization that includes a variety of approaches, measures, criteria, perspectives, audiences, and even interests. Evaluation is no longer solely based on technical and analytical techniques, and increasingly favours negotiation.

Approaches and Methodologies: -

Curriculum evaluation methods have an impact on practise and have evolved in tandem with curriculum changes. Measurement and the collection of factual data defined some early curriculum evaluations. A psychometric approach was prevalent, with a focus on evaluating student achievement rather than policies and procedures. Teachers and schools were evaluated on their ability to deliver the curriculum via tests.

Tyler (1949) popularised the targets accomplishment curriculum model as a response to the focus on traditional content curriculum. This progression paralleled the modernization of industry. Tyler's objectives model looked at the curriculum from a behavioural standpoint, evaluating it in terms of student accomplishments and outcomes. This approach to curriculum evaluation focused on inputs and outputs, included pre- and post-testing, and experimental design, and appealed to the common man since it was straightforward and straightforward. The model's shortcomings were quickly found. Teaching to the test was one of them, as was a lack of concern for the quality of the objectives.

Curriculum and pedagogy issues were rarely addressed in such evaluations, and questions about why certain objectives were not met were not addressed. The curriculum, in terms of teaching and learning activities, remained the black box in this evaluation technique.

Critics of the objectives attainment model of review quickly arose, with Scriven (1967) centering evaluation on determining the goals' validity or worth, as well as whether the programme was truly meeting the client's needs. He defined formative and summative evaluations, as well as the duties (functions) and goals (what needs to be accomplished) of evaluation. According to Scriven, evaluation included value judgements and target achievement estimations.

Cronbach (1981) weighed in on the topic, emphasising the importance of usability above accuracy in evaluation criteria for improvement, particularly when looking into the causes and effects of teaching quality. Cronbach was one of the first to use evaluation data to improve a course or serve a formative purpose.

On the one hand, this matrix provides the data gathering structure for the evaluator to attend to the intents and observations for description, and on the other hand, the standards and decision making for judgement. Stake believed that in order to evaluate a programme, it needed to be described as well as judged. The notion of time was captured in this assessment model by segregating the antecedent, transaction, and outcome data.

This methodology is more responsive to challenges raised by different people in the programme, and it constitutes a step forward, especially methodologically, toward a more process-oriented approach. The impetus and emphasis are provided by the teaching and learning programme in the framework of curriculum evaluation. There is recognition of the audience's various information needs.

Interpretation of Evaluation Data

Data Evaluation

The designation of a research goal, the presence of a research question, the type of methodology, data gathering processes, sample information, data analysis methodologies, and study findings were all part of the data evaluation.

The method for analysing and interpreting evaluation data will be primarily determined by the type of data collected and how it will be used and presented (e.g., as part of a journal article and report, or as an instant representation of feedback about an activity at a public event such as a physical chart, an online graphic or via social media).

Data from storey evaluations has been used in a variety of ways, including:

- For research purposes, statistical study of online usage for use in journal publications, presentations, and impact statements.
- Thematic analysis of post-launch interviews in reports, in order to investigate longer-term perspectives on the resource and its impact on teaching practise, as well as to support funding applications.
- In teaching sessions, presentations, journal articles, and promotional materials, storyteller quotations and testimonials are used to demonstrate the rationale for producing the resource and the motivation of storytellers to share their experiences.

Data Interpretation

Data interpretation is the application of procedures for viewing data in order to arrive at a well-informed judgement. The interpretation of data gives the information studied a meaning and determines its significance and ramifications.

The significance of data interpretation is obvious, which is why it must be done correctly. Data is likely to come from a variety of sources, and it has a tendency to arrive in the analysis process in a random order. Data analysis is notoriously subjective. That is to say, the nature and objective of interpretation will differ from one company to the next, and will most likely be related to the data being studied.

However, before any meaningful data interpretation investigation can begin, it is important to understand that visual representations of data findings are meaningless unless a clear judgement about measurement scales is made. The scale of measurement for the data must be decided before any significant data analysis can begin, as this will have a long-term impact on data interpretation ROI. Among the several scales are:

- **Nominal scale:** - non-numerical categories that can't be ranked or compared in any way. Variables are both exclusive and exhaustive in their scope.
- **Ordinal scale:** - exclusive categories having a logical order that are both exclusive and exhaustive. Ordinal scales include things like quality

ratings and agreement ratings (i.e., good, very good, fair, etc., OR agree, strongly agree, disagree, etc.).

- **Interval:** - a measurement scale in which data is organised into groups with equal distances between them. An arbitrary zero point is always present.

How to Interpret Data

When evaluating data, an analyst must strive to distinguish between correlation, causality, and coincidences, as well as a variety of other biases, but he must also evaluate all of the elements that may have contributed to the outcome. One can employ a variety of data interpretation techniques. The purpose of data interpretation is to assist people in making meaning of numerical data that has been collected, evaluated, and presented. Your analyst teams will have a framework and consistent foundation if they have a baseline method (or methods) for analysing data.

Indeed, if separate departments take different techniques to interpreting the same data while working toward the same goals, misaligned goals might arise. Diverse approaches will result in duplication of work, inconsistency in answers, wasted energy, and, ultimately, time and money. We'll look at the two basic types of data interpretation in this section: qualitative and quantitative analysis.

Qualitative data interpretation

In a nutshell, categorical data analysis is qualitative data analysis. Data is described in qualitative analysis using descriptive context rather than numerical values or patterns (i.e., text). Narrative data is typically obtained through a number of person-to-person procedures. Among the approaches used are:

- **Observation:** - describing the behavioural patterns observed in a group of people. The length of time spent on an activity, the sort of activity, and the form of communication used could all be examples of these patterns.
- **Focus group:** - To develop a collaborative discussion about a study issue, group people and ask them relevant questions.
- **Secondary research:** - Different sorts of documentation resources can be categorised and divided based on the type of material they include, similar to how patterns of behaviour can be detected.
- **Interviews:** - one of the most effective approaches for gathering narrative data Themes, topics, and categories can be used to group

inquiry responses. The interview method enables extremely targeted data segmentation.

In the interpretation stage, there is a clear distinction between qualitative and quantitative analysis. Because qualitative data is so subject to interpretation, it must be "coded" to make grouping and classifying data into distinct themes easier. Qualitative data analysis is generally described by three basic principles: notice things, collect things, and think about things. This is because person-to-person data collection approaches can often result in debates over correct analysis.

Quantitative data interpretation

If there was a single word to describe quantitative data interpretation (and there isn't), it would be "numerical." When it comes to data analysis, there are few guarantees, but you can be sure that if the research you're doing doesn't involve numbers, it's not quantitative. Quantitative analysis is a set of procedures for analysing numerical data. It frequently requires the application of statistical modelling techniques such as standard deviation, mean, and median. Let's take a brief look at some of the most commonly used statistical terms:

- **Mean:** - The term "mean" refers to the numerical average of a group of responses. A mean represents the middle value of a set of numbers when dealing with a data set (or many data sets). It's the total number of values in the data set divided by the total number of values in the data set. Arithmetic mean, average, and mathematical expectation are other names that can be used to express the notion.
- **Standard deviation:** - This is a statistical phrase that is frequently used in quantitative analysis. The standard deviation displays the response dispersion around the mean. It describes the consistency of replies and, when combined with the mean, provides insight into data sets.
- **Frequency distribution:** - This is a metric for determining the frequency with which a response appears in a data set. Frequency distribution, for example, can be used to determine the number of times a certain ordinal scale response appears in a survey (i.e., agree, strongly agree, disagree, etc.). When it comes to establishing the degree of agreement among data points, frequency distribution is quite important.

Quantitative data is typically measured by visually presenting correlation tests between two or more significant variables. Different procedures can be combined or utilised independently, and comparisons can be made to get a conclusion. Other quantitative data interpretation procedures that have their own distinct signatures include:

- **Regression analysis:** - Regression analysis is a technique for determining the relationship between a dependent variable and one or more independent variables based on historical data. Knowing which variables are interconnected and how they have evolved in the past allows you to predict potential outcomes and make better decisions in the future. For example, if you want to forecast your sales for the coming month, you may use regression analysis to figure out what factors will influence them, such as sales, the introduction of a new campaign, and so on.

- **Cohort analysis:** - This approach finds groups of users who have similar features over a period of time. Cohort analysis is often used in business to understand distinct client habits. A cohort, for example, could be all users who signed up for a free trial on a particular day. An investigation would be conducted to determine how these users act, what activities they take, and how their behaviour differs from that of other user groups.

- **Predictive analysis:** - The predictive analysis method, as its name suggests, seeks to forecast future changes by studying historical and current data. Predictive analytics approaches, which are powered by artificial intelligence and machine learning, allow firms to notice patterns or possible challenges ahead of time and prepare educated initiatives.

- **Prescriptive analysis:** - Prescriptive analysis, which is also based on predictions, use techniques such as graph analysis, complex event processing, and neural networks, among others, to try to understand the impact of future actions so that they can be adjusted before they are made. This aids in the development of adaptable and viable corporate strategies.

- **Conjoint analysis:** - The conjoint technique is commonly used in survey analysis to determine how people value distinct aspects of a product or service. This aids academics and businesses in determining price, product qualities, packaging, and a variety of other characteristics. Menu-based conjoint analysis is a typical application in which people are given a "menu" of possibilities from which to create their ideal concept or product. As a result, analysts can determine which traits they prefer above others and draw conclusions.

- **Cluster analysis:** - Last but not least, cluster analysis is a technique for categorising items. Cluster analysis is a great tool for uncovering hidden trends and patterns in data because there is no target variable. Clustering is commonly used in market research to identify age groups, geographical information, and earnings, among other things. In a business context, it is used for audience segmentation to create targeted experiences, and in market research, it is often used to identify age groups, geographical information, and earnings, among other things.

Now that we've seen how to interpret data, let's move on to some questions: what are some of the advantages of data interpretation? Why do all industries engage in data research and analysis? These are fundamental inquiries, but they don't always get the attention they deserve.

Need and significance of Curriculum Evaluation

Significance: -

We can use evaluation to see if what we're doing is effective. If it isn't, it can assist us in determining how to improve, adapt, and ensure that it is. It allows us to keep going forward and being productive. In the field of medical research, review is ongoing until a solution that is as safe and effective as feasible is discovered. That assessment can assist us choose medications that benefit us rather than those that don't and have too many serious side effects. In any other field, evaluation is essential. It's futile to accomplish anything without some sort of assessment. Otherwise, we won't be able to progress.

Need of curriculum evaluation: -

The requirement for curriculum evaluation stems from the necessity for both instructors and students to assess the extent to which their current curricular programme and implementation have resulted in good and curricularly appropriate outcomes for pupils. Examine a significant section of the curriculum that is being assessed.

Any national education system must include curriculum evaluation as a required and significant component. It serves as the foundation for curriculum policy decisions, input on ongoing curriculum modifications, and curriculum implementation processes. The accomplishment of educational programme goals and objectives.

Helps with learning experience selection: Curriculum development is required for the proper selection and arrangement of learning experiences. It aids in the selection of study materials and other activities so that students can achieve the educational goals and objectives.

References: -

- https://socioed.wordpress.com/.../18/88-concept-of-curriculum-transaction/
- https://www.sciencedirect.com/topics/social-sciences/curriculum-evaluation/
- https://theintactone.com/2021/09/26/data-evaluation-and-interpretation/
- https://www.datapine.com/blog/data-interpretation-methods-benefits-problems/
- https://www.quora.com/What-is-the-significance-of-evaluation-in/
- https://colors-newyork.com/why-there-is-a-need-to-evaluate-the-curriculum/

CHAPTER VIII

Curriculum and Indian Education System during Vedic Period

****Mrs. Madhurima Chaudhuri (Majumder)**

• • •

Introduction:

A nation's system of education is an integral part of its culture and value system. The ancient India had her distinctive culture and civilization of over thousands of years. In the past the great saints had played a decisive role in shaping and molding the ancient heritage. A system of education reflects the life of a nation, its character, its socio-political and economic conditions as well as aspirations. The distinctive identity of the people which we call 'national character' influences national culture and education. The main aim of education in India was to develop various aspects of life and also to ensure social service.

The culture and education of anation does not simply reflect the nation's past. It reflects the present values, demands and needs of life too. It looks forward and shows the path to the future. In India, history of education began with the Vedic period.The ancient Indian education emerged from the Vedas. The Vedas are the best expression of an enlightened culture and have contained within themselves the seeds and sources of Hindu thoughts and practices.

According to Rig Veda, "Education is something which makes a man self-reliant and selfless."

According to Upanishads, "Education is that whose end product is salvation."

According to Vedantic point of view, "The essence in man is spirituality. We need education that quickens, that verifies, that kindles the urge of spirituality inherent in every mind".

The aims of Education in Vedic period were as follows:

- To realise the supreme and achieve supreme consciousness.
- Inculcation of spirit of piety and righteousness.

- Preservation and spread of ancient culture.
- To unfold the spiritual and moral powers of individuals.
- Perfection of the physical, mental and intellectual personality of the students.
- Formation of good and moral character.
- Inculcation of social and civic duties for a better future life.

Curriculum:

Curriculum played an important role in Vedic education system. It was dynamic and not static. The fundamental goal of building a good curriculum was to develop students physically and mentally.The curriculum was basically organized on the firm foundation of the Vedas, Vedangas, and Vedantas in succession. Gradually, however,itaquired more masses and diverse interests including secular and popular studies. Specialisation came into vogue and differential curricula were organized for the different castes. Teachers became specialized to feed the specialized schools. Professional and vocational education befitting the different castes was standardized. Moreover, theory and practice went together. There was no formal education for the Sudras and Vratyas. They received practical training in their family trade and profession as members of the family production units. Curriculum during Vedic education was linked with the following aspects:

- Vedas: Rigveda, Yajurveda, Samaveda and Atharvaveda.
- Puranas
- Spiritual aspects: Soul, Self, God, Divinity of nature etc.
- History and stories based upon important aspects of life and personalities
- Arithmetic and Geometry
- Astronomy
- Philosophy
- Logic
- Ethics
- Conduct
- Rituals
- Understand and implementation of Vedic aphorism
- Medicine (Ayurveda)
- Military Science

- Agriculture
- Animal Husbandry
- Arts and crafts
- Construction
- Sculpture
- Commerce and Trade
- Yoga
- Administration
- Diplomacy

The Gurukul had its annual calendar as well as the daily time table. Working days, study hours, time and methods were prefixed. Natural calamities, inauspicious phenomenal signs or other reasonable grounds led to suspension of studies for the day.

System of Education:

The education system that prevailed during the Vedic period had some unique characteristics. During this period students used to live away from their parents, their education comprised of subjects like physical education, mental education, politics, economics etc. The medium of language was Sanskrit. They were shaped in a way that they can live in any condition considering how difficult the situation will be. Education was confined to the upper castes and to those who were 'Brahmacharis'. The children of the upper castes like brahmin, kshatriya or baishya used to initiate their education after performing a ceremony known as Upanayan that is taking child to the guru for the purpose of education. Guru used to give Guru Mantra to the students and then start his education. Shudras were not allowed for education.

During those times the education was of Vedas, Brahmanas, Upanishadsand Dharmasastras. From the Rigveda onwards, our ancient education started with the objective of developing the students not only in the outer body but also on the inner body. The ancient education focused on imparting ethics like humanity, truthfulness, discipline, self-reliance and respecting all creations to the students. The education was mostly imparted in Ashrams, Gurukuls, Temples, Houses.Sometimes Pujaris of temples used to teach students. The education system of ancient India had some special features and uniqueness which was not found in any other ancient education system of the other countries. The education was mostly given in forests under the blue sky which keeps the student's mind fresh and alive.

During ancient time people used to lead a simple life and doing their work with devotion and hard work.

There were differences on the fixation of age for initiating education in the Ashram of a Guru. The age for Upanayan Ceremony might be eleven or twelve years.

The general duration of education was twelve years. Only one type of Veda could be studied during the span of twelve years. Students used to select one Veda out of four for their education.

Gurukul system of education is very prominent feature of Vedic education. Students used to live in the Ashram of Gurus for the purpose of education. Gurukuls were situated in natural surrounding and away from cities.

In Vedic period student life was as under:

- Meal was provided only two times, morning and evening. There was no provision of food in-between because it is not good for health as well as spiritual development.
- There were different dress codes for the students of different castes.

- Students were supposed to be disciplined and self-controlled.
- They used to get up early in the morning.
- They were required to perform morning and evening prayer.
- 'Havan' was an important activity.
- Respect for teachers.
- Not allowed for telling lies and passing any unexpected comment against anyone.
- Students were restricted to keep money with them.
- Brahmacharya was very important for them.
- They were instructed to control sex, anger and greed.
- They were not allowed to purchase anything.
- Students were supposed to lead a simple life.
- They were not allowed to talk about their caste, wealth, position etc.
- They used to live under common living conditions of the Ashrama.

Method of Instructions:

In Vedic period the teachers paid special focus on their students and taught them according to their knowledge and skill level. Teaching was basically through verbal and debate based. Since Knowledge had to be delivered through mouth, received by the ear and preserved in memory, the art of recitation with proper accent, sound and pronunciation was perfected. Yet it was not simply learning by rote in the ordinary sense of the term. Learning by heart without conceptual understanding was considered worthless. The truth had to be realized. This required concentrated thinking and meditation leading to revelation. Doubts were cleared by intelligent questions and answers. Moreover, wisdom was not a matter of intellect only. It required concentrated feeling and being. Hence, precondition to real wisdom was annihilation of doubts and worldly illusion, which could be attained through self-control, Yoga and Sannyas. Obviously, Yoga was simultaneously the road to discipline, morality and absolute knowledge.Following methods of teaching were used during this period:

- Recitation method
- Discussion method
- Question-Answer method
- Memory methods
- Illustration with examples
- Pronunciation method
- Meditation method
- Storytelling method
- Apprenticeship

Teacher-Student Relationship:
In Vedic period, teacher and student developed a value and intimate relation between them. Teacher or the guru was used to be a spiritual personality.Guru was equaled with Brahma, Vishnu and Maheshwar. He was given very revered position and treated with respect and honour throughout. Teacher and students lived together in the Ashram. He was the parent of his disciples in his Ashram. There was a direct contact between the guru and students. Students completely submitted themselves to the guru. Students used to contact gurus and receive education as per their perceptionof education. Routine duties were generally performed by the students while living with the gurus. Teacher/guru used to teach and make general arrangement for students for required life style. The teacher was deeply involved with the students and understood all his strengths and weaknesses. He looked towards all-round development of his students. He used to be encouraging in his attitudes. Teacher used to be scholar in many

areas like, Philosophy, Methodology of acquiring knowledge, Grammar, Astrology and many other subjects. Teacher used to behave with students as their own children. Students were very obedient to every command and wish of the teacher. Connection of student-teacher was on a one-to-one basis. Teacher used to develop the personality of the students in accordance with aims of education. Teacher used to develop in students a desire of education. They were taught to realise their responsibilities towards parents, society and the guru. Teacher used to teach social skills to the students.

A student had to live this rigorous life for twelve years which was generally the period of formal studenthood.Of course, informal studenthood was a lifelong process. In this case self- study was the method. The Samabartanai.e, Convocation was held at the end of twelve years if the teacher thought that the student was fit for graduation.Snatakasi.e, graduation was of three types- i) Vidya Snatakas, who had attained intellectual proficiency. ii) VrataSnatakas, who had attained perfection in practices. iii) Vidya -VrataSnatakas, who excelled in both theory and practice. The Snataka left the gurukul, but acquired further intellectual proficiency by participating in debates, discussions and assemblies.

Conclusion:

Vedic system of education focuses on the all-round development of students. More emphasis was given to practical knowledge rather than theoretical knowledge. The students were not just involved in bringing the ranks, but their main focus was on knowledge. Classrooms were made in forests which provide a pleasant study environment to the students. There was no pressure laid on students related to studies so that they can learn effectively. The government did not interfere with the formation of curriculum, rather helped in the development of education.

Some disadvantages are found in this system of education. The students led a hard life without any personal choice or liking. The education was basically oral and the written texts were missing.Women were not admitted to the gurukul. Because of caste system all children of different castes were not allowed in gurukul.Lastly, we may conclude that the Vedic education being mostly spiritual, liberal and contemplative in nature, was meant for all who were really interested, capable and dedicated and were in search of the highest truth and supreme knowledge.

References:

- Gandhi Kishore, Issues and choices in Higher Education: A sociological analysis, B.R

  Publishing Corporation, Delhi, 1977.

- Joshi, R.N.: Education- Elsewhere and Here, Bharatiya Vidya Bhavan, Bombay, 1979.
- Lakshmana Swamy Mudaliar A.: Education in India, Asia Publishing House, Bombay,

  1960.

- Majid Rahnema: Educational Strategies in Developing Countries, Sterling Publishers,

  New Delhi, 1976.

- Rao, V.K.R.V.: Education and Human Resource Development, Allied Publishers,

  Bombay, 1966.

Analysis of ICT Preference of Teachers for Transacting the Curriculum at Higher Secondary Level

****Dr. Archana S.S**

• • •

Abstract

Information and Communication Technologies has turn out to be regular entities in all aspects of human life. The needs and demands of the 21st century encouraged the use of ICTs into classroom situations. ICT expands knowledge retention and engagements in the field of education. The capacity of ICT to customize the educational programs to meet the needs of individual learners leads its universal acceptance in curriculum transaction. It provides different opportunities to make learning more fun and enjoyable. The present study analyzed the ICT preference of teachers for transacting the curriculum at Higher Secondary Level. The findings revealed that majority of the teachers (76%) preferred Instructional Technology as an effective ICT for transacting the curriculum at Higher Secondary Level.

Key Words: Curriculum Transaction, Information and Communication Technology, Instrument Technology, Instructional Technology, Dissemination Technology.

Introduction

Curriculum Transaction is the effective and anticipated implementation of the curriculum contents on the basis of aims and objectives enumerated in the curriculum. Curriculum transaction denotes teaching of the content of various subjects and the practical work to be done in each area of the study as prescribed. A curriculum is a tool, it has to be transacted if learning has to takes place. Transaction consists of the process of putting into practice the set of activities enlisted or of covering the topics given in the curriculum. It weighs a considerable amount of reflection, visualization and planning. It incorporates effective planning for providing learning experiences for its learners. Hence, it needs utmost operation of all available resources-physical, material, financial and human for its efficient and effective transaction.

The 21st century, the age of information and technology (IT) demands every aspects of life to be connected with technological novelties. The massive flow of information is occurring in all fields throughout the world. In educational field, information and technology is prevalently making teaching -learning process successful and interesting for teachers and students. As the classroom changed its traditional look, teachers need to cope -up with different technology for using them in the classroom for making teaching-learning more interested. Information and Communication Technology become an appropriate tool for effective implementation of student-centric methodologies. It ensures classroom discussion active by making it two-way communication.

ICT act as the gateway to the world of information and helps teachers to be updated. It creates awareness of advanced trends in instructional methodologies and evaluation mechanisms. It enables better and swifter communication and presentation of ideas more effective and relevant way. ICT expands the opportunity for communication and collaboration among students themselves, as well as teachers and students. It offers an opening for teaching to be student-centered. It rises student enthusiasm for learning by encouraging students to search more information from multiple sources and affords the ability to use a variety of digital resources for learning purposes. ICT creates an open learning environment that allows information and materials to be stored and used as many times as needed.

Information and Communication Technology are of vital importance in all levels of education system. The well-organized use of ICT implies the transfer and use of all types information, with an importance on the role of communication and the integration of telecommunication, computer technology and audio-visual systems, which let users to access, store, transfer and use information (Sharma, 2014). Information and Communication Technology involves a group of innovative technologies used for the rapid growth of intellectual and economic potential of strategic resources, ensuring sustainable development of societies that generate innovation in teaching and also have made a radical change when compared to the old teaching-learning paradigm (Bilialova, 2017; Damodaran and Rengarajan, 2007). The goal of integrating ICT in curriculam is to make the learning process efficient, gorgeous and up-to date (Haji, Moulayonge& Park , 2017), which has brought about radical changes in the education system and facilitates their acceptance, make teaching more robust and connects it with the world (Ismailova & Ergashev, 2019).

Information and communication technology has been recognized as a catalyst for educational change because it is able to change work situations, access, handing and exchange of information and introducing innovations in teaching and learning approaches. ICT offer a variety of technological equipment and resources used to generate, communicate, distribute, collect and store information.

Information and Communication Technologies (ICTs)

Information and Communication Technology is a comprehensive notion including both information technology and Communication Technology. As information technology covers those technologies that help in processing, organizing and storage of information. Communication technologies cover technologies that enable dissemination of information. With the advent of internet technologies, the use of information technology and communication technology has become blended due to blurring of the dividing line. Thus, ICT is an umbrella term that can be defined as technologies capable of handling information and tools to process, organize, produce, store, distribute and generate knowledge and to enhance capabilities of human beings.

ICT can be of three types (Wadi D. Haddad, 2007) as Instrument Technology, Instructional Technology and Dissemination Technology.

1. **Instrument Technology**

Radio, Television, Computer, Compact- Disc player etc. comes under instrument technology. Selecting an instrument for educational purpose involves decision about educational goals, classroom methodologies, role of teacher, role of student, modalities of group work, role of text book and external sources of knowledge. These ICTs in school require supporting infrastructure that include electricity, communication, wiring and special facilities. For introducing TVs, radios, computers into school must be followed by sufficient curriculum-related content ware. The development of content software that is integral to the teaching learning process is a must. It should develop in accordance with its curricular and instructional framework.

1. **Instructional Technology**

Classrooms are constrained environments and conventional instructional materials are static. Audio, video, animations, taped classrooms, digital texts, PowerPoint, transparencies, multimedia comes under instructional technology. Instructional technologies provide tremendous potential to the teaching - learning process that can animate, stipulate, capture reality and can add movements to the concepts.

3. Dissemination Technology

Technology can disseminate information through various techniques such as broadcast radio, broadcast TV, social networks, websites, Online Reference Services, QR codes etc. Technology is the most effective tool for sharing the knowledge instantly and people are able to access information quicker and easier than ever before. Regardless of the platform preferred academicians, scientists and researchers use this tool to promote their work and share information with learners.

Need and Significance of the study

ICTs bring novelty factors to motivate the learners to study. It distributes learning resources in varieties of format depending on the necessities of the subject. Teachers entails more knowledge and confidence with ICT and an improved understanding of its possibilities helps pupils to make learning more enjoyable. Extensive support for continuing professional development is essential for the teachers to integrate these technologies and infuse ICT matters in curriculum transaction. The most effective use of ICT is those in which the teacher and the software can challenge pupils understanding and thinking (Ghosh, 2006). If the teacher has the skill to unify and stimulate the ICT- based activity can ensure effective whole class and individual works. With rich inputs, ICTs can enable learning experiences more situated as well as authentic to improve the quality of learning. To effectively infuse and integrate ICT into teaching and learning, teachers need to use a range of practices that are crucial to the pedagogical frame works (Goel, 2003). ICTs today play a substantial role in training as well re-training of teachers and there by updating their knowledge and skills to provide quality support to the learners. ICT change teaching and learning through its possibilities as a source of knowledge, a medium to convey content, a resource of collaboration and discussion. But the pedagogical practices of teachers using ICTs can have brief improvements because of their inclination towards traditional method of teaching. ICTs should be employed for curriculum transaction in order to provide quality education to the students. It is the need of the hour to analyze the ICTs used for transacting the curriculum. Need and significance of the study is hence justified.

Statement of the Problem

The effective use of ICT has great impact on teaching and it absolutely changing the role of the teacher in classroom as a facilitator. It enables students to work, learn and research independently. This improve and modernize the teaching process, making it more efficient by introducing more sensory components into information flow. The use of ICT strategy in curriculam transaction primarily depends on the teacher, as its level and efficiency of innovating the teaching process is greatly determined by the teacher's knowledge on ICT, level of digital skills, incidence of using ICT for educational purposes and teachers' attitude towards the use of ICT. Hence, the present study is entitled as *"Analysis of ICT Preference of Teachers for Transacting the Curriculam at Higher Secondary Level"*.

Objective

To analyze the ICT preference of teachers for transacting the curriculam at Higher Secondary Level.

Hypothesis

There exists difference in the ICT preference of teachers for transacting the curriculam at Higher Secondary Level.

Methodology

Method

The investigator adopted survey method for the study as it affords opportunities for determining the predominant conditions and it is essentially a technique of quantitative description of the characteristics selected for the study. Since, the present study aims to find out ICT preference of teachers for transacting the curriculam survey method was found suitable.

Population

The population of the study involves Higher Secondary School Teachers.

Sample

Sample selected for the study consists of 50 teachers working at different Higher Secondary schools of Thiruvananthapuram and Kollam districts of Kerala state.

Tool used for the Study

The investigator developed a questionnaire consists of 30 questions on three categories of ICTs namely, Instrument Technology, Instructional Technology and Dissemination Technology. Ten questions were provided for each category. The questions were all Yes/No types.

The procedure adopted for the study

The present study is online based. The questionnaire was administered to the sample through google form. The completed forms were analyzed by using suitable statistical techniques.

Analysis and Interpretation

The data collected were analyzed quantitatively by calculating the percentages. The details of the analysis are presented in Table. I

Table. I

ICT preference of teachers for transacting the curriculum at Higher Secondary Level

ICTs	Number	Percentage
Instrument Technology	08	16
Instructional Technology	38	76
Dissemination technology	04	08

From Table1, it is obvious that, out of the total sample {N=50}, majority of the teachers (76%) preferred Instructional Technology for transacting the curriculum at Higher Secondary level where as 16% of the sample preferred Instrument Technology and only 8% of teachers favored Dissemination Technology for transacting the curriculum at Higher Secondary Level.

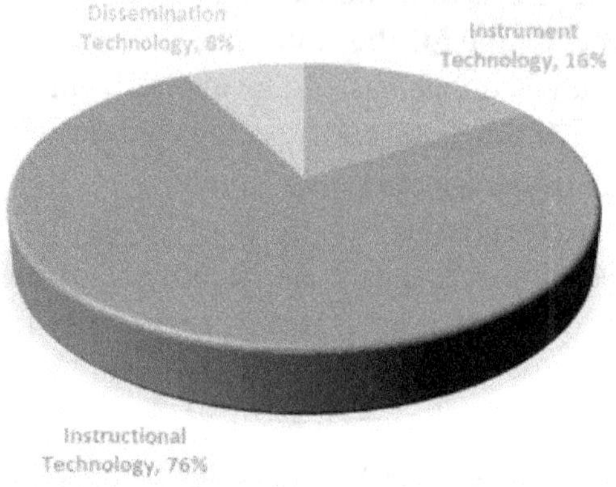

Figure I:ICT Preference of Teachers for Transacting the Curriculum at Higher Secondary Level

The tenability of the Hypothesis

Acquiring Knowledge and skills in the field of ICT is one of the prerequisites for teachers in the modern society. ICT should be utilized for curriculum transaction to ensure and promote quality learning among students. ICT-based teaching expands the range of cognitive tasks which enables the paradigm shift to systematic management of teaching activity. The knowledge, skills and interests of teachers on ICT greatly influences their selection and use of appropriate technologies for curriculum transaction. The hypothesis proposed *"There exists difference in the ICT preference of teachers for transacting the curriculum at Higher Secondary Level"* is hence accepted.

Major Findings

- There exists difference in the ICT preference of teachers for transacting the curriculum at Higher Secondary Level.
- Instructional Technology is the most preferred ICT for transacting the curriculum at Higher Secondary Level.

Suggestions

Use of ICT for transacting the curriculum will change the ways in which knowledge is represented. It will challenge pupils understanding and promote greater thinking and reflection. Teachers can effectively transact the curriculam by understanding the relationship between a range of ICT resources and the concepts, processes and skills in their subject. ICT-mediated learning has long lasting influence upon the students. But, in many schools, teachers are not well trained to transact the curriculum using ICT. Their initial training, often the only one they have received, generally does not include the preparation of teaching materials or the use of contemporary technologies for teaching. Most teachers are unwilling to invest substantial amounts of their own time and resources in bringing their knowledge and competencies up to date in these areas, and few school systems provide incentives for this to take place. Teachers should be empowered and trained with high quality educational videos and software to understand the relationship between a range of ICT resources and the concepts, processes and skills in their subject. It will develop confidence in them to prepare and plan lessons using ICT resources.

Conclusion

Curriculum transaction is the effective implementation of lesson plans in classrooms. It has been found that ICT has significant role to play in refining the standards of the teaching-learning process. It provides variety of resources for the presentation of content which helps learners in concentration, better understanding and long retention of information. The effective use of ICT has great impact on teaching and is definitely changing the role of the teacher in the classroom. Teachers should be trained properly to select appropriate ICT resources in the classrooms. It will enable the learners to acquire ICT knowledge, skills and awareness to be successful in their futures. ICT has the potential of endorsing jobs and entrepreneurship and contributes much to socio-economic development of the country.

References

- Bilialova, A. (2017). ICT in Teaching a Foreign Language in High School. Procedia-Social and Behavioral Sciences, 237, 175-181. https://doi.org/10.1016/j.sbspro.2017.02.06
- Damodharan, V. S., & Rengarajan, V. (2007). Innovative methods of teaching. In Learning Technologies and Mathematics, Middle East Conference (pp. 1-16). Muscat, Oman: SultanQaboosUniversity.

- Ghosh, A. 2006. Communication Technology and Human Development. New Delhi: Sage.
- Goel, D. R. (2003), ICT in Education, Changes and Challenges in ICT in Education. M. S. University, Baroda.
- Vanaja, M. & Rajasekhar, S. (2009), Educational Technology and Computer Education, Neelkamal Publications Pvt. Ltd., Hyderabad.
- Haddad, W. D. 2007. ICT for Education: A reference handbook,www.ictineducation.org.
- Haddad, W. D. & Draxler, A. (Eds). 2002. Technologies for Education. Paris: UNESCO.
- Haji, S. A., Moluayonge, G. E., & Park, I. (2017). Teachers' Use of Information and Communications Technology in Education: Cameroon Secondary Schools Perspectives. Turkish Online Journal of Educational Technology
- Ismailova, Z., & Ergashev, B. (2019). New information and communication technologies in education system. In E3S Web of Conferences, 135 (pp. 1-8), EDP Sciences. https://doi.org/10.1051/e3sconf/201913504077
- Jamir, C., & Pongen, M. (2021). The role of information and communication technologies in improving teaching and learning processes in higher education: Bridging the gaps.
- Sharma, Ajay (Jun. 2014) Curriculum transaction procedures in Secondary Teachers 'Pre-
- Service training programme of Himachal Pradesh: An Evaluative study Himachal
- Pradesh University, Shimala, India.

CHAPTER X

Difference between Curriculum & Syllabus, and Role of State in Curriculum Construction

Mrs. Sanchita Mazumdar,*Mrs. Runa Guha, ****Mr. UdayModak

• • •

Introduction

Definition of Curriculum

The curriculum is defined as the guideline of the chapters and academic content covered by an educational system while undergoing a particular course or program.

In a theoretical sense, curriculum refers to what is offered by the school or college. However, practically it has a wider scope which covers the knowledge, attitude, behaviour, manner, performance and skills that are imparted or inculcated in a student. It contains the teaching methods, lessons, assignments, physical and mental exercises, activities, projects, study material, tutorials, presentations, assessments, test series, learning objectives, and so on.

Definition of Syllabus

The syllabus is defined as the documents that consist of topics or portion covered in a particular subject. It is determined by the examination board and created by the professors. The professors are responsible for the quality of the course. It is made available to the students by the teachers, either in hard copy or electronic form to bring their attention towards the subject and take their study seriously.

A curriculum also helps in planning how a certain subject or course will be taught while the syllabus just includes topics and concepts that will be covered. We often use them as interchangeable terms without knowing that they are entirely different. *The distinction between curriculum and syllabus is that a subject syllabus is simply a component of a course or subject curriculum. Curriculum is a combination of the syllabus, course design, class schedule, and lesson plans for the subject.* Before pursuing an academic program, you can understand its structure in a more detailed way if you know the difference between syllabus and curriculum. So, let's begin with the discussion of syllabus vs curriculum and explore their key differences.

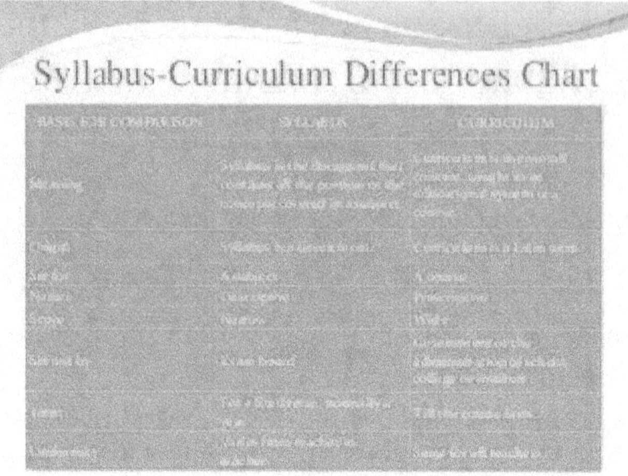

slideshare.net

Difference between Curriculum and Syllabus:

1. The curriculum is the overall content, taught in an educational system or a course. But Syllabus is a document that contains all portions of the concepts covered in a subject.
2. The curriculum is a Latin term. But Syllabus is a Greek term.
3. Its main aim is all round development of the learners. But its main aim is to achieve the specific objectives of instruction.
4. The curriculum is a Course. But Syllabus is descriptive in nature.
5. The curriculum is perspective in nature. But Syllabus is descriptive in nature.
6. It means overall aspects of all the content areas. But it means course of studies.
7. The curriculum has a wide range of scope. But Syllabus has a narrow range of scope.
8. The curriculum is a broad based term. It is used in general to denote the overall content of the Educational system. But Syllabus is much more specific with respect to Curriculum.
9. Curriculum construction or prepared by Government or administration, (Bodies, Agency e.g.-UGC, NCTE, NCERT, SCERT, CBSE, ICSE,) of

School, College or institute. But Syllabus construction or prepared by Examination cell or board.

10. The curriculum's duration is till the lasts. But Syllabus's duration is for a fixed term, normally a year.

11. Uniformity of Curriculum is same for all teachers. But Uniformity of Syllabus is varies from teacher to teacher.

12. There are no specific time limitations for the completion of Curriculum. But there is specified time for the completion of syllabus.

13. It provides all the formal and informal activities that take place during the interaction of the learners and teachers. But it provides the details of the content of the study.

14. Curriculum consists of curricular, co-curricular and extra-curricular activities. But Syllabus is a part of curriculum. It only consist of curricular content and related activities.

Role of State in Curriculum

Introduction:

The term 'State' thus means a group of people occupying a definite territory, organized under a Government and who are subject to no outside control. Woodrow Wilson giving a very simple and matter-of-fact definition says that the State is a "People organized for law within a definite territory."

State is an association and brings about co-ordination among various agencies.It is well-organized part of the society in a systematic and effective manner.It not only ensures peace and order in the society, but also promotes general well-being and prosperity of the human being. State, in fact, maintains and develops the human culture and civilization through ages.

Objectives of the Study:

1. The study wills emphasis the various importance and historical perspective of role of state in Curriculum.

2. To highlight various ways to create such an awareness about Concept of Curriculum construction among young and future generation in our society.

3. The study will suggest the opportunities and scenario of role of state in Curriculum construction for future generation in our Nation.

4. The study will discuss about the various benefits and advantage of Curriculum construction associated role of state.

5. The study will conduct how we can promote the factors affecting the curriculum transaction.

Historical Perspective:

Providing education is an important function of the State. Education prepares citizens for the State. Thus education and state are mutually related and one for other. Close relationship between state and education could be seen even in the ancient Greece.

In Sparta, one city-state of Greece, education was controlled by the State. Another city-state of the times was Athens where democracy was most important and education was provided for preparing its children for citizenship. The autocratic rulers like Hitler of Germany and Mussolini of Italy also provided as well as controlled education according to their policy and principles. Education was subordinate to the State.

The scenario of state in curriculum construction in independent India:

India is a multicultural society made up of numerous regional and local cultures. People's religious beliefs, ways of life and their understanding of social relationships are quite distinct from one another. All the groups have equal rights to co-exist and flourish, and the education system needs to respond to the cultural pluralism inherent in our society.

Curriculum development has a broad scope because it is not only about the school, the learners and the teachers. It provides answers or solutions to the world's pressing conditions and problems, such as environment, politics, socio-economics, and other issues on poverty, climate change and sustainable development.

The followings are the roles of State in Curriculum Construction:

A. **Policy Making:**

Normally, the state doesn't directly construct curriculum, but it put forth the policies for different sections and levels of education.

A. **Construction of Bodies:**

The state constructs official bodies at different for construction of curricula for different courses and programmes offered at diferent levels. Different levels of such bodies are – (a) National Level, (b) State or Province Level and (c) University Level or Board Level.

C. Appointment of Members:

The state appoints members of different such bodies, strictly following the criteria for the selection such as the qualification, experience in the field, etc.

The criteria for the appointment are:-

- Experience in the educational field.
- High Qualification.
- Research Skills on Curriculum Construction.
- Multisided Vision.
- Knowledge in Psychology & Sociology.
- Innovative Nature.

D. Providing Guidelines for Curriculum Framework:

The state provides guidelines for curriculum framework in the following dimensions:-

- Aims of the curriculum.
- Major focused areas.
- Duration for different courses.
- Hours to be allotted per day or per week.
- Special mention in Selection of Contents.

E. Monitoring the Enacted Curriculum:

The state also monitors the enacted curriculum by doing the following things –

- Construction of Supervising Team.
- Providing Guidelines to the Team.
- Decentralizing duties to the different sections of the Team.
- Immediate action on the Report submitted by the Team.
- Providing facilities to the Team.

F. Ensuring Resources for Enactment of the Curriculum:

The state ensures the resources for enactment of the curriculum in the following aspects :-

- Ensuring human resources.
- Ensuring material resources.
- Flexible procedure for purchasing new materials.
- Immediate Actions for maintenance.
- Organizing meetings of headmasters/headmistresses.

G. **Assessment of Existing Curriculum:**

The state not only ensures human resources for enactment of the existing curriculum but also asses the existing curriculum by the help of the following :-

- Collecting feedback from all the stake holders.
- Systematic Analysis of the Feedback.
- Checking the Validity and Reliability of Feedback.

H. **Revision and Reconstruction of Existing Curriculum:**

The major role of state in respect to curriculum construction is the revision and reconstruction of curriculum in terms of societal needs. The major tasks associated with this process are -

- Construction a curriculum revision committee.
- Giving due regard to the feedback from the Stake Holders.
- Observing the changes occurred in the Educational field.
- Observing the changes occurred in society.
- Rendering freshness to the curriculum.

Conclusion:

Generally, the state does not directly make curriculum but it put forth the policies for numerous sections. The Central Government helps the states for educational development in following ways,

Central Government makes educational functions through NCERT, UGC, Central Universities, Central Schools organizations, (CBSE, etc.

References:

- Dr. Jayanta Mete, Parthita iswas, Pranay Pandey-"Knowledge and Curriculum'- Rita Book
- Agency.
- Dr. Kaushik Chakrabarti & Rekheebrita Biswas-Knowledge and Curriculum- Aahali Publishers.
- Dr. Sujit Pal, Kayal Kundu, Sourovi Thakur-"Knowledge and Curriculum"-Aahali Publishers
- https://keydifferences.com/difference-between-syllabus-and-curriculum.html#:~:text=The%20syllabus%20is%20described%20as,is%20
- same%20for%20all%20teachers.
- https://leverageedu.com/blog/syllabus-vs-curriculum/

Foundations And Principles Of Curriculum

Dr. Savita Mishra,*Divine Tomar

• • •

Introduction

Foundation of Curriculum

Curriculum Foundations The influences that shape curriculum developers' thinking are known as foundations. As a result, they have an impact on the curriculum's content and organisation. The curriculum represents a country's society and culture, and it is a society's wish that its children learn the habits, ideas, attitudes, and skills of adult society and culture, and educational institutions are the best means to transmit these skills. Teachers and schools have the responsibility of disciplining society's youth and providing them with a set of experiences in the form of curriculum. The needs, knowledge, and information of society serve as the foundation for curriculum development.

www.graduateprogram.org

The foundations of the Curriculum are:

Philosophical Foundation

Beliefs are the focus of the Philosophical Foundation. Philosophy is the pursuit of knowledge; it is the search for everlasting truth, reality, and general life principles, not just plain truth. Curriculum aids in the application of information in real-life situations and the comprehension of life's realities and concepts, which is why it is referred to as the dynamic side of philosophy. Curriculum is used to change students' conduct, and philosophy aids in the process of creating new ways and foundations for teachers and curriculum planners to change students' conduct.

Philosophy also aids in the exploration of new teaching approaches and how to apply them in the classroom to improve the teaching-learning process. It also introduces new approaches and methodologies for assessing student achievement and curriculum evaluation. Philosophers of the past have had a significant impact on clarifying the relationship between the nature of knowledge and the process of curriculum development, as well as providing a foundation for curriculum; Plato presented a curriculum in his book "Republic" at the time, and it is still the core of today's curriculum. In human life, knowledge is given a prominent position.

Education philosophy and ideology give norms and principles that guide decision-making in educational practises and policy development. It aids in the promotion of human life through social change in student behaviour by guiding the curriculum planner on the basis of the society's philosophical and ideological beliefs in the construction of subject matter while keeping in mind future expectations and needs of the schools.

Sociological Foundation

The curriculum in schools is influenced by society. Every society, town, or nation has a social responsibility to plan for children's education. Curriculum influences social change, and curriculum influences social factors. A good curriculum should not only focus on the current social situation, but also address how learners should prepare themselves to deal with shifting social forces.

Curriculum development is influenced by sociological factors in the following ways:-

It gives a means of modifying student behaviour in accordance with the needs and desires of society or nation.

- To use education as a tool for social change and advancement.
- To keep the culture alive and pass it on to the next generation.
- To prepare students for the society of the future.

As a result, sociological considerations provide crucial guidelines for building a viable curriculum for societal improvement and advancement. As a result, curriculum planners must consider social aspects and how they might be used to plan for and enhance social responsibility. As curriculum planners, we must consider current societal characteristics as well as anticipated future social characteristics.

Psychological Foundation

Education is for the benefit of the child. The educational process revolves around the child. In the teaching-learning process, these psychological concepts serve as a foundation. To be effective, a teacher must have a thorough understanding of child psychology.

Efforts are made through education to bring about desired changes in the learners' behaviour. Psychology, being a behavioural science, is intertwined with the educational process. It aids curriculum developers in determining what information and learning experiences should be included. It establishes the foundations for curriculum development in such a way that curriculum can be tailored to the needs of children in a particular grade. Because psychology explains how a person learns, it is critical to understand the psychological foundations of curriculum. Because the teaching-learning process occurs between live beings, psychology is necessary to provide an example.

The psychology of individual differences among children has an impact on curriculum planning and development. As a result, the curriculum should be varied and flexible enough to accommodate individual variances, requirements, and interests. As a result, we can deduce that the theories put up by psychologists (Piaget, Erickson, Bruner, etc.) from time to time guide curricular development. As a result, the psychological foundations for curriculum development are sufficient.

Principle of Curriculum Construction

Curriculum principles are the values a school believes will give both their pupils and community the best chance of succeeding, and what they know to be right, given its context. You can think of curriculum principles as being like those by which you live your life and base important decisions on. Except, when deciding on curriculum principles, a school needs to consider what will give all its children the best possible chance of becoming informed, well-rounded, happy individuals who are prepared for the next steps of their lives.

Having clear curriculum principles gives the staff of any school a unity of purpose. But what factors might help a school to decide upon them? Influencing factors might include all or some of the following: personal values, religious beliefs, social context, geographical location, pedagogy, national policy, and resources.

You will need to decide which of these factors are important to your school and how to balance them. Amanda Spielman's initial commentary on curriculum states that, for some schools, external pressures such as school inspection or KS2 tests have led to a 'focus on performance' trumping the urgency to establish and stick to a set of fundamental principles, although, she says, not intentionally.

www.cornerstoneseducation.com

The main principles of curriculum construction may be mentioned as under:

Principle of Child-Centeredness .

The focus of the curriculum should be on the children. It should be based on the child's needs, requirements, and circumstances. More experience is required of the child than instruction. Because the modern educator is focused on the child, the curriculum should likewise be focused on the child. It should be determined by the child's interest, aptitude, age, and circumstances.

In any curriculum design concept, the child should be at the centre. The most important goal of curriculum is to guide a child's growth in the appropriate direction so that he or she may adapt successfully in life.

Principle of Community -Centeredness

We should not just regard each child as an individual but also as a member of the community to which he belongs. In reality, as a citizen, the learner will be an engaged member of the community. It is, therefore, highly desirable that his needs and desires coincide with the wants and desires of people with whom he must live. Though the child's development and growth is the primary focus of the curriculum, his social behaviour must also be appropriately developed; both the child's individual and social development require equal attention. He must be able to live in and contribute to society.

As a result, the curriculum must represent the values, attitudes, and skills that exist in the community. The society, on the other hand, is not static. It's alive and well. With the rapid progress taking place in many industries, its needs and requirements are changing. This is an important issue to consider when working on development.

Principle of Activity-Centeredness Action

It's an indication that you're alive. Man is a living creature. As a result, the curriculum should include a variety of physical and mental activities in which youngsters are naturally interested. The activity should be linked to the child's wants and requirements, as well as societal and educational integration principles. The curriculum should be centred on the diverse activities of students. It should give carefully selected activities based on children's general interests and developmental phases. It should include activities that are productive, creative, and project-based. Play activities for little children should also be provided.

Purposeful activities should be provided both inside and outside of the classroom. The required experiences can be supplied through a web of activities, and as a result, beneficial behavioural changes in children can be achieved.

Forward Looking Principle

Education's goal is to educate a youngster for a successful adult life. As a result, the curriculum should provide insight into the child's future existence. The goal of education is to prepare a child for a successful social existence. As a result, the curriculum should not be tailored solely to the child's current needs. It's also important to think about what he'll need in the future. The curriculum should also incorporate knowledge, skills, experiences, influences, and other factors that will improve a child's ability to make effective adjustments later in life.

Conservative Principle

The human race's traditions and culture should be preserved and transmitted through the curriculum. It should include subjects, ideas, or activities that encourage pupils to value and appreciate their own traditions and culture. The preservation and transmission of our cultural legacy is one of the most important functions of education. This is critical for human advancement. Traditions, conventions, attitudes, skills, behaviour, values, and knowledge are all part of culture. However, curriculum creators must make an appropriate selection of cultural elements, taking into account their educational worth as well as the developmental stage of the students.

Principle of flexibility and Variety

The Secondary Education Commission (1953) proposed that secondary school curricula give variety and flexibility. Modern curricula should be built in accordance with local and individual demands and circumstances. In order to meet the demands of each individual, the curriculum must be varied.

Learners should have the option of choosing their own subjects. Learners should not be pressured into enrolling in a programme of study. Individual differences between students must be taken into consideration. Rapid advancements are occurring in a variety of disciplines in our time. As a result, society's needs are in jeopardy.

The content of the curriculum cannot remain the same in the future. It should not be in a stagnant state. It must be dynamic and adapt to changing circumstances. It should be up to date in terms of educational and psychological trends. The curriculum should be broad in scope in order to meet the demands of a diverse range of students, allowing them to choose subjects and activities based on their abilities and interests.

Students' needs differ from one location to the next. Students in rural, urban, and hilly settings, for example, will have distinct demands. Boys and girls have different requirements. As a result, the curriculum should incorporate these factors.

Principle of Coordination and Integrity

The integration principle is critical for the development of a child's overall personality. Various courses included in the curriculum at a given level of school, such as history, civics, geography, and social studies, should be integrated. The integration principle should be used to organise various operations. Naturally, the students will be exposed to a variety of experiences through various disciplines and activities, but they must be nicely integrated. Various disciplines and activities must all work toward the same end goal: the accomplishment of educational objectives.

The activities and subjects should not be separated into compartments, but should be interconnected and fully integrated to help the child develop as a whole.

Principle of Conservation

The preservation and transmission of our cultural legacy is one of the most important functions of education. This is critical for human advancement. Traditions, conventions, attitudes, skills, behaviour, values, and knowledge are all part of culture. However, curriculum creators must make an appropriate selection of cultural elements, taking into account their educational worth as well as the developmental stage of the students.

PPrinciple of Creativity

The preservation of culture contributes to the society's long-term viability. Culture should not only be passed down, but also nourished. The curriculum should include provisions for developing a child's creative abilities so that he can become a contributing member of society. "There must be certainly creative themes in curriculum that is tailored to the requirements of today and tomorrow," Reymont argues.

Principle of Balance

Curriculum should be functional rather than decorative. It should not be limited to issues that are rooted in tradition. Students must be able to apply the material in real-life situations. As a result, technical and vocational education should be included in the curriculum. It's important to remember the many principles of curriculum development. Various regional and national circumstances should also be taken into account. In reality, all variables that will aid in the achievement of educational goals should be taken into account.

Principle of Maturity and Utility

The curriculum should be tailored to the student's mental and physical development.

The curriculum should be useful to the students and so preserve a vocational and technical grounding. Work experiences should be prioritised. Curriculum should be functional rather than decorative. It should not be limited to issues that are rooted in tradition. Students must be able to apply the material in real-life situations. As a result, technical and vocational education should be included in the curriculum. It's important to remember the many principles of curriculum development. Various regional and national circumstances should also be taken into account.

In reality, all variables that will aid in the achievement of educational goals should be taken into account.

References

- https://www.owlgen.in/what-athe-sociological-foundations-of-curriculum-development/
- https://physicscatalyst.com/graduation/bases-of-curriculum/
- https://www.yourarticlelibrary.com/education/curriculum-construction-in-india-education/84842
- https://www.slideshare.net/ParvathySalim/principles-of-curriculum-73284888
- https://www.preservearticles.com/education/the-main-principles-of-curriculum-construction-may-be-mentioned-as-under/18040
- https://www.owlgen.in/discuss-about-psychological-foundations-of-curriculum-development/

CHAPTER XII

Curriculum Development: A Method of Curriculum Enhancement

****Tanwangini Sahani**

• • •

Introduction

Curriculum refers to the lessons and academic content taught in a school or in a particular course or programme. Curriculum is sometimes defined as the courses offered by a school in dictionaries, but it is rarely used in schools in this broad sense. Curriculum typically refers to the knowledge and capabilities that students are expected to learn, which includes the learning standards or learning objectives that they are expected to meet; the units and lessons that teachers teach; the assignments and projects that students are given; the publications, materials, recordings, presentations, and readings used in a course; and the exams, evaluations, and other criteria for assessing student performance.

Figure 1: www.iconteach.com

Teachers often construct their own curricula, which they refine and improve over time, but they often adapt lessons and syllabi established by other teachers, utilise curriculum templates and guidelines to plan their classes and courses, and buy prefabricated curricula from individuals and companies. Teachers are often forced to utilise or follow extensive, multigrade curriculum packages—often in a specific subject area, such as mathematics—that schools acquire. Curriculum can also include a school's graduation criteria, such as the courses students must take and pass, the number of credits they must earn, and other requirements, such as completing a capstone project or completing a particular number of community service hours.

Due to the sheer importance of curriculum creation in formal education, the curriculum has evolved into a dynamic process as our society changes. As a result, curriculum refers to the "whole learning experiences of individuals not only in school but also in society" in its broadest definition. Curriculum development is defined as a method for making beneficial changes in the educational system that is planned, deliberate, gradual, and systematic. Every time there are changes or developments in the world, it has an impact on school curricula. It is necessary to update them in order to meet the needs of society. Curriculum development is vast in scope since it encompasses more than just the school, the students, and the teachers. It also has to do with the evolution of society as a whole. Curriculum development is critical in today's modern economy for a country's economic growth. It also offers answers or remedies to the world's most important concerns and difficulties, such as environmental dangers, political issues, socioeconomic problems, and other issues relating to inequality, environmental issues, and sustainability. To establish a society, a sequence of developmental processes is required. First, the school curriculum, particularly in higher education, must be developed to protect the country's national identity while also ensuring the expansion and stability of the economy. As a result, a nation's leader should have a compelling view for his country and its people.

Objectives

- To Understand Stages of Curriculum Development
- To Know Challenges of Curriculum Development
- To Learn about Three Models of Curriculum Design

Analysis and Discussion

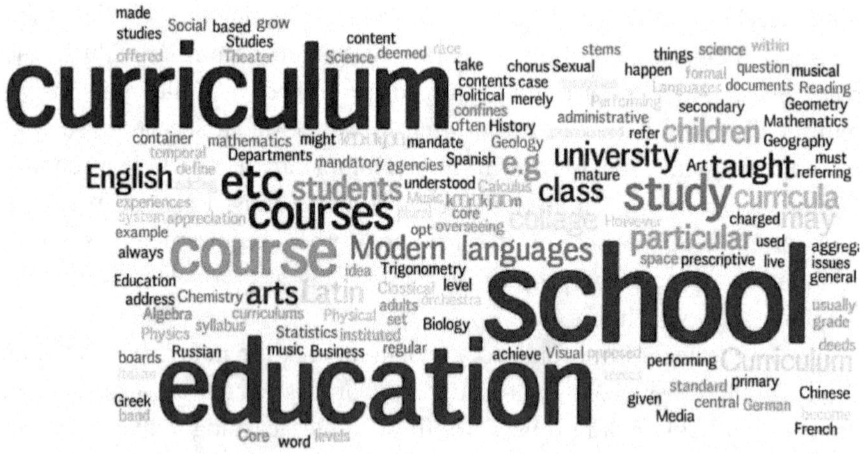

Figure 2: seven-senses.nu

Various decisions are taken when establishing either a teaching/learning unit or a unified curriculum in order to create a realistic curriculum that incorporates all of the elements of effective curriculum. The procedure for planning a unit or a whole curriculum is to break down the systematic steps in order to ensure orderly thinking, to allow for a systematic study of the elements that compare such a plan, and to allow for a precise and cautious research and application of the notifications issued and facts.

The processes for creating a unit or curriculum are as follows:

Step 1:Planning

The specific development steps are written out during this stage. A curriculum development team is formed after the idea or topic being addressed is determined. Once the professionals have been collected, they examine developments in the content area and assess the students' requirements.

Step 2: Content

As the team enters the second stage, their focus shifts to the curriculum's targeted results, the program's unifying structure, and the content they're concentrating on. Following that, new ways for teaching the material are developed.

Step 3: Implementation

Finally, the new procedures and designs are implemented. Facilitators must be thoroughly taught on the new curriculum, and any changes should be made in response to feedback. Because not every design achieves the desired objectives, developers must be willing to adapt.

Step 4: Evaluation

As the curriculum is used, it may need to be updated as the world changes. It's possible that new stuff will be added, while old content will be removed. Furthermore, with newer groups of students, the curriculum may begin to fail, necessitating a change.

Challenges of Curriculum Development

Curriculum development is not a straightforward or easy procedure because there are so many phases to follow. Additionally, instructors at all levels of education may confront extra challenges that make the process more complex or time-consuming. Amongst challenges are the following:

- **Institutional Requirements:** You may be required to follow standards established by your state's board of education or by the institution's management. This could include covering material that will be tested through standardised assessments, as well as incorporating product-focused curricular aspects. It could also mean including specific course objectives.

- **Experts in Development Face Long Waits:** Your institution's curriculum experts may be on staff to assist professors with course preparation. Unfortunately, demand is frequently much higher than these tiny teams' capacity, resulting in lengthy wait times.
- **Gathering Relevant Required Materials:** Instructors will need to find the proper essential materials to correspond with course objectives once the curriculum is basically outlined. It's often difficult (and often impossible) to locate a cost-effective choice that also works well for your course. This is all too often the case with traditional publishers' textbooks and e-textbooks, but emerging possibilities like personalised digital course materials can help ease these worries.

Many teachers may believe they aren't up to the effort of establishing an excellent curriculum on their own due to the numerous hurdles and intricate steps needed. In this scenario, a professional course material creator could assist in streamlining and simplifying the procedure.

Three Models of Curriculum Design

- **Subject-centered curriculum design:** It is focused on a specific topic or discipline, such as mathematics, literature, or biology. The subject, rather than the student, is the focus of this curriculum design concept. It is the most widely used model of standardised curriculum in K-12 public schools. Teachers create subject lists that include particular examples of how they should be studied. This style is most commonly seen in big university or college classes where lecturers concentrate on a single subject or discipline.

Lists of subjects and precise examples of how they should be studied are compiled by teachers. This style is most commonly encountered in big university or college classes when lecturers concentrate on a single subject or discipline. In comparison to other types of curriculum design, subject-centered curriculum design is not student-centered, and the approach is less concerned with individual learning styles. This can lead to issues with student involvement and motivation, as well as a drop-off in pupils who aren't sensitive to this paradigm.

- **Learner-Centered Curriculum Design:** It, on the other hand, focuses on the needs, interests, and goals of the students. It recognises that children are not all the same and should not be forced to follow a standardised curriculum in all situations. This strategy tries to give students more control over their education by allowing them to make decisions. Differentiated instructional plans allow for the selection of timely and relevant assignments, teaching and learning experiences, or activities. Students have been found to be engaged and motivated by this type of curriculum design. The disadvantage of this type of curriculum design is that it can put pressure on teachers to develop content that caters to students' learning requirements and preferences. In a mostly online learning setting, these insights can be difficult to come by.

- Problem-centered curriculum design: It instructs students on how to analyse a problem and come up with a solution. Because students are exposed to real-life situations and abilities that are transferable to the real world, a problem-centered curriculum approach helps them participate in authentic learning. Problem-centered curriculum design has been found to improve curriculum relevance and foster creativity, innovation, and collaboration in the classroom. The disadvantage of this technique is that it does not always accommodate for students' specific needs and interests.

Recommendation and Findings

Figure 3: /www.ncreduservices.com

- The University and each college should be encouraged to include the goal of preparing students for citizenship in a technological and information-rich society in their mission statements. Students must be able to access, use, and analyse information that is relevant to their vocations and lives as citizens, as well as communicate and collaborate successfully using current technology tools.

- The curriculum committees of each college should establish the information and technology capabilities students should have to accomplish the college goal, with some support from the University. The committees should also make sure that the curriculum is structured to assist students meet the needed competences in each circumstance.

- Individual institutions should engage in strategic planning processes for the continuing integration and management of technology in the instruction they provide, with wide representation from the campus community. Taking a broad (and long) view of both the role of instructional technology in a college's curriculum and the need for faculty development and training efforts is the best way to clarify both the role of instructional technology in a college's curriculum and the need for faculty development and training efforts.

- In order to coordinate work with instructional technology and support cross-campus initiatives, the University should engage in strategic planning/management as an ongoing process with broad representation from the University community.

Conclusion

To summarise, no curriculum will be perfect, a finished work etched in stone, or free of criticism, but it must be accepted by instructors and recognised educationally valid by parents and the general public in order to be effective. Curriculum development should be considered as a process in which students' needs are met and their learning is improved. It also can't be in a state of stagnation. Curriculum must be a live document that is updated on a regular basis. It must be flexible enough to adapt to changes in the educational community and society at large. Then and only then will it be able to be an effective educational change agent. Better use of 'change knowledge' is required for successful curriculum development. Neglecting it is a common cause of failure. Policymakers, educators, and instructors all need to learn more about the factors that influence curricular change in schools. As a result, any real curriculum reform effort should include learning about educational change and its fundamental components.

At all levels of curriculum development and review, it is critical that the teacher be involved. This will ensure that quality control is carried out at all phases of the development process. As a result, the teacher can be confident that all components of the curriculum have all important information, such as the course goal, aims and objectives, justification, entry requirements, evaluation, and assessment, among other things. Any curriculum should ensure that schools and higher education programmes are delivered in the most efficient and current manner feasible. When examining a curriculum subject, a teacher should be able to think about how to address the recognised requirements of students within educational facilities or programmes. The curriculum should also include a technique for assessing the quality and completeness of its components, such as instructional concepts, functional knowledge, self-perceptions, attitudes, skills, and duration. It will aid in determining the degree of faithfulness between the curriculum and its implementation in the classroom, as well as assessing the curriculum's influence on students' knowledge, attitudes, and behaviour.

References

- The Meaning and Importance of Curriculum Development, https://simplyeducate.me/2014/12/13/the-meaning-and-importance-of-curriculum-development/Alvior, Mary G., December 13, 2014
- Curriculum Development and the 3 Models, https://tophat.com/blog/curriculum-development-models-Amanda Stutt, February 25, 2021
- 95.STAGES IN THE PROCESS OF CURRICULUM DEVELOPMENT, https://socioed.wordpress.com/2016/10/16/95-stages-in-the-process-of-curriculum-development/, Dr. C. Praveen, October 16, 2016
- The Four Stages of Curriculum Development, https://lauriekimbrel.wordpress.com/2016/07/06/the-four-stages-of-curriculum-development/, Laurie Kimbrel, July 6, 2016
- Curriculum Development: Teacher Involvement in Curriculum Development, https://files.eric.ed.gov/fulltext/EJ1095725.pdf
- Curriculum Development, https://www.ukessays.com/essays/education/curriculum-development.php

CHAPTER XIII

Evaluation of the Curriculum

**Ms.Rashima Sharma

• • •

Introduction

Evaluation of the Curriculum

The previous modules in this block dealt with curriculum creation and its implementation in higher education. Curriculum evaluation is necessary for the planning and development of educational procedures. It is the process of determining the efficacy of a curriculum in terms of goals and what has been accomplished. Midway through the programme, student progress is monitored to ensure that teachers are fulfilling instructional I objectives on time. Teachers will be in charge of the monitoring role. When the curriculum is finished, it is evaluated. This is done using a multi-pronged approach to see if the material and technique have resulted in pupils gaining the requisite knowledge and abilities. Teachers must question themselves if their students are reaching their expectations on a regular basis.

Potential outcomes of learning:

• define curriculum evaluation in a higher education environment;

• Describe the various stages of curriculum evaluation during the development of a curriculum.

• Examine the many needs, sources, and aspects of curriculum evaluation at the higher education level.

Level of schooling; and

• make recommendations about how to acquire evaluative data.

Overall evaluation of a curriculum indicates:

Teacher

Student curriculum

Curriculum, in its broadest sense, is a system of learning experiences that are purposefully developed and carried out in order to achieve specific objectives. Evaluation is a systematic procedure for assessing and appraising a system's or practice's proficiency level. The proficiency level is determined by comparing what the system or practise has accomplished to what it was expected to achieve in light of its goals. As a result, curriculum evaluation entails systematically assessing and quantifying the appropriateness and efficacy of learning activities at a given level. A thorough examination of the course provides insight on the content selection and sequencing, as well as the teaching and assessment methods used. The major goal of evaluation is to improve the course for future students.

Curriculum Principles

The term "curriculum" refers to both formal and informal school activities. School life does not have to be limited to the four walls of the school, but can extend far beyond that. The importance of the curriculum in the educational process cannot be overstated. The following are the fundamental principles of curriculum development.

i) Totality of Experiences Principle: First and foremost, it must be understood that, according to the best modern educational thought, curriculum in this context does not refer only to the academic subjects traditionally taught in schools, but also to the totality of experiences that students gain through a variety of curricular, co-curricular, and extracurricular activities.

ii) Child-Centeredness Principle: When developing a curriculum, the nature, concern, motive, and need of the child should be taken into account first. The child is the focal point around which all of the school's curricular activities revolve and develop. The curriculum should be altered to bring the child closer to the pre-determined curriculum rather than the child bringing the pre-determined curriculum closer to the child.

iii) Conservation and Creative Principle: An effective curriculum must be founded on the conservation and creativity principles. We should incorporate concepts and experiences in the curriculum that aid in the preservation of cultural heritage. In light of changing demands and situations, they should be able to be modified further. A static curriculum is impossible in today's world. Subjects that allow the youngster to use his constructive and creative abilities should be included in the curriculum.

iv) Integration Principle: The curriculum should not be divided into separate academic subjects. Various disciplines included in the curriculum at a given level of education should be integrated and associated with a variety of other subjects as well as the students' daily lives.

v) Flexibility Principle: In order to meet the many needs and concerns of individuals and society, it is necessary to be flexible. The flexibility and dynamism of the curriculum should be emphasised. It should enable for desired content changes and alterations from time to time from time to time in order to maintain it's current.

vi) Character Formation Principle: The curriculum's goal is to help pupils build their character and personalities. It should instil in them ideal character traits and qualities through a set of rules, laws, and routines. Affective education should be included in the curriculum for this character development.

vii) Mental Discipline Principle: One of the key tasks of curriculum is to develop the learner's various mental faculties or capacities for efficiency and precision. Individual mental abilities are acquired through cognitive effort and experience.

Evaluation Tools and Techniques

The process of Continuous and Comprehensive Evaluation relies heavily on evaluation tools and procedures (CCE). The information received must be interpreted in a clear and concise manner.

Scores, grades, and qualitative phrases are all used. Not just any judgments should be made in CCE. On scholastic components, as well as co-scholastic aspects, which are heavily reliant on learning. An institution's ambiance and learning culture In terms of interpretation, success can be defined as be assessed at several stages.

• With regard to the learners' current state of progress, strengths, and learning objectives voids, etc.

• The projected level of learning in relation to the criteria, taking into account the required abilities.

• Tools are basically data and information gathering equipment. Questions, for example.

• Tools include things like observations, tests, inventories, record or document analysis, and so forth. In this case, the tools.

• CCE, on the other hand, necessitates settings in which it can be used. For example, observation as a tool necessitates scenarios such as debating a competition, participating in a project activity, and so on. A teacher can keep an eye on a student.

Assessment can be done with a variety of tools. There are two types of assessment tools: standardised and non-standardized, which are as follows:

Standardized tools have objectivity, reliability, validity, and quality of information. Determining whether a person is a high or low performer. Validities of several types, e.g. Concurrent validity, construct validity, and content validity Ensure that there is a sense of balance and relevancy. The ability to move quickly is a must. Some tests use it as a factor, although it isn't used in all of them. Psychological evaluations and intelligence and aptitude tests, as well as interest and study habit inventories; Attitude scales, for example, have those characteristics.

Teacher-made assessments, rating scales, and observation schedules are examples of **non-standardized tools.** Schedules for interviews, questionnaires, opinionnaires, and checklists, among other things.

Some of the tools and techniques are:

(1) Question Method

The most popular method of determining what youngsters know, think, envision, and feel is to ask them questions. A professor, during the process of teaching, becomes aware of learning challenges in one of his students.by posing questions to them Questions are primarily used as a tool. During the examinations important information must be included in the questions.

Characteristics of Question Method

1. **Objective-based:** A question should be based on a pre-determined goal and structured in such a way that it successfully assesses the goal.

2. **Instructions:** Through the instructions, it should specify a certain task.

Appropriate directing phrases and structured scenarios should be used to accomplish this.

3. **Scope:** In accordance with the estimated time and marks assigned to it, it should identify the limit and scope of the answer (length of the answer).

4. **Content:** The questions should assess the same content area as the one being assessed.

5. **Language:** An excellent question is written in clear, concise, and unambiguous language that the students can understand.

6. **Difficulty Level:** When writing a question, take in mind the level of the students for whom it is intended. The question's difficulty is determined by the skill being assessed, the content area being tested, and the amount of time available to answer it.

7. **Power Analysis:** A good query should analyse the differences between the bright students and the rest of the pupils.

8. **Scope of the Answer:** The question's phrasing should be specific and precise such that the desired answer's scope is clearly specified.

9. **Value Points:** A question's total value points or marks, as well as its subparts, should be clearly stated.

Types of Question Method

The answer may vary from one word to several paragraphs. Such types of questions are also called as 'free - response' questions. Supply - type questions may be divided into four categories as follows:

1. **Essay-style questions:** An essay is a written response that is a long piece of writing. The student is given complete flexibility in terms of wording, length, and organisation of the response. A distinction should be noted between the essay type question used to measure knowledge and the writing task, which is an essay type question intended to test writing skills in languages. These abilities are:

• Choose relevant facts from the body of knowledge you've accumulated. Establish linkages between various aspects of knowledge and identify them.

• Weigh the evidence in light of the implications of the acquired data.

• To derive inferences from facts and other sorts of information by organising, analysing, and interpreting them.

• Take a unique or indigenous method to solving an issue.

• Support one's point of view with facts, evidence, and persuasive arguments. Examine the adequacy, accuracy, and relevance of the information available in a specific scenario critically.

• Recognize a problem on both a big and micro scale.

• Conceive, design, and propose new and inventive solutions to a specific problem.

2. **Constructing Essay-Type Questions:** Essay-type questions typically begin with words like "discuss," "explain," "evaluate," "define," "compare," "contrast," "describe," and so on. When the number of people being assessed is small and there is only a limited amount of time to prepare for the test, essay-style questions are a viable option. It's also ideal for evaluating written expression.

3. Short Answer Questions

Short answer questions have the following characteristics:

• They may be used profitably in all assessments

• They can be used to test practically all educational objectives

• They assist students acquire the ability to organise and select relevant data.

• It may be judged more objectively than essay-style questions, ensuring consistency. Because multiple questions can be added in place of one - essay style question, these questions help to cover more curriculum.

4. Short Answer Questions: Short answer questions have a single testing point and can be graded very objectively. These questions allow for more content to be examined, as well as increased reliability and validity. It aids in the examination of the examinee's knowledge by requiring them to offer a term, phrase, figure, or sentence that is needed to answer the questions. It can be replied in a single sentence or in a single word. It usually takes one to two minutes to respond, and the maximum score is one point. All educational topics can benefit from the usage of very short answer questions.

5. Objective Type Questions: Students must respond to these questions by selecting the proper answer from a list of options. These can be classified as alternative answer, matching, and multiple choice questions, among others.

(2) Observation Method

Observation can be used to gather information on a child's behaviour in natural settings both within and outside of the classroom. Other data can be gathered by observing students performing activities and tasks in a planned and purposeful manner.

The following are some of the benefits of using observation techniques.

• Identify and recognise the various facets of a student's personality development.

• Recognize and distinguish between people and groups.

• Recognize and recognise on a regular basis throughout a period of time.

• Using a 'on-the-spot record,' recognise and identify the kids' performance and understanding.

• Over time, a pattern of interests, aptitudes, and other characteristics emerge, forming a complete portrait of the learner.

• Concerns and hazards associated with observation as a method for assessment.

• Making snap judgments based on a single or a few observations.

• The observer's ability to determine "what" is being observed.

• The method the observation is conducted lacks sensitivity and objectivity.

• Observations in a single circumstance rather than spanning time, activities, and environments.

In a variety of settings, observations can be utilised as an assessment method. Debates, elocution, group work, practical and laboratory activities, projects, play fields and school prayers, clubs and festivals can all be utilised. While observation can be biased and subjective, utilising an observation plan can significantly reduce such errors and hazards.

(3) Inventories and tests

Oral tests should not be used to assess information or abilities that can be assessed through a written exam. Because oral tests are one-on-one, they take longer than group writing assessments. Where a student struggles with written expression, oral assessments are most suited to assess the depth of learning. Oral examinations and testing.

- Allow the student to take part in the learning evaluation.
- Assist in the evaluation of listening and speaking abilities.
- Evaluate verbal skills such as fluency, expressiveness, and correctness.
- Probing questions are used to assess the pupils' understanding depth.

Oral tests necessitate preparation as well.

(4) Checklist

The concept of a checklist was introduced earlier under the heading of questions. Checklists, on the other hand, can be utilised in a variety of other assessment situations. For example, whether a kid can dress appropriately for the occasion or boldly address the students during the school prayer are examples of life skills. When the answer is either 'yes' or 'no,' a checklist is employed. There's a chance you'll get mixed up. Checklists can only be completed by gathering information through observation, inquiry, or document analysis. As a result, a checklist is primarily used for data recording and documentation.

(5) Rating Scale

When a response or learner behaviour is expected to be on a scale from excellent to poor, or from satisfactory to unsatisfactory, a rating scale is used.

(6) Anecdotal Record

The term 'anecdotal records' comes from the word 'anecdotes,' which refers to small events and episodes. An anecdotal record is a description of a student's observed behaviour. It's a record of an important event in the student's life that shines light on his or her behaviour, thinking, talents, and abilities, exposing significant aspects and qualities about his or her personality.

(7) Document Analysis

In research, record or document analysis is frequently utilised. The importance of this technique is in the assessment of pupils based on documents such as assignments, projects, journals in science, geography, and other fields. In certain ways, this method is also used to assess responses to essay-style inquiries. To support the notion and its explanation, the accessor searches for and recognises the major points, arguments, illustrations and instances, derivations and numerals, and so on.

(8) Portfolio

A portfolio is a compilation of proof of a student's work throughout time. It could be day-to-day tasks or a selection of the student's best work. Portfolios are frequently used by painters and commercial artists to demonstrate their abilities and quality work prior to being selected.

9) Competitions and Quizzes

Quizzes and competitions are commonplace in today's electronic media, particularly television. This type of evaluation is almost always positive. In addition to checking the participants' knowledge, it aids in the development of collaboration and teamwork in group events.

10) Assignments

Open-ended or structured projects based on a theme to be done as classwork or homework. Some may be based on situations that aren't covered in textbooks.

Conclusion: Curriculum evaluation is the process of using scientific processes to acquire valid and reliable data in order to make decisions regarding a curriculum that is now in place or has been adopted. Curriculum evaluation, in simple words, can be equated with research because it employs systematic study, scientific procedures, and research methods.

Essentially, the curriculum assessment process is used to determine whether or not learning programmes such as intra curricular, extracurricular, and co-curricular have been implemented in teacher-developed learning. Furthermore, the output resulting from the implementation of the curriculum programme in the form of learning must correspond to the curriculum's original objectives.

References:

- curriculumevapdf,
- https:/sncourseware.org,
- www.teachersadda.co.in,
- https://notesread.com,

CHAPTER XIV

Curriculum and Pedagogic Structures of School Education as per NEP2020

** Dr. Rajat Dey

• • •

Introduction:

In 2015, the Central government set up a committee headed by Late Shri T.S.R. Subrmanian to observe the need for reforms and propose a new education policy. In 2019, the committee submitted its draft under the chairmanship of Sri K. Kasturiranjan, and was called the 'New Education Policy 2020. The NEP is expected to over haut the Indian education space completely. The NEP, as defined by the centre, is egalitarian in nature, which will lead to a vibrant knowledge society. It seeks to instil such skills, values and dispositions in an individual that world ensure sustainable development, global well-being and world form a global citizen.

Transforming Curricular & Pedagogical Structure:

The Curricular and pedagogical structure of school education will be reconfigured to make it responsive and relevant to the developmental needs and interests of the learners at different stages of their development, corresponding to the age range of 3-8, 8-11, 11-14 & 14-18 years respectively.

Therefore the new pedagogical and curricular structure of school education will be guided by 5+3+3+4 design, consisting of the following stages-

• **Foundational Stage (Grades 1-2, Covering age 3-8 Years):**

Learning items in the formative years are developing curiosity, logical thinking & problem solving, arts, crafts & music, relationship with nature, colours, and shapes, alphabets & numbers, teamwork & collaboration, play based & discovery based learning, ethics, self identity and etiquette, behaviour & emotional development. This stage is consist of

a. 3 Years of Angarwadi or Pre-School and
b. 2 Years of primary school in Grades 1-2;

both together covering ages 3-8 years. This stage consists of flexible, multilevel, play or activity- based learning.

- **Preparatory Stage (Grades 3-5, Covering age 8-11 Years):**

The Preparatory stage will comprise 3 years of education building on the play; discovery and activity- based pedagogical and curricular style of the foundational stage. It will also begin to incorporate some light text books, interactive classroom learning in order to lay a solid ground work across Subjects, (reading, writing, speaking), physical education, art, language, science & mathematics.

- **Middle Stage (Grades 6-8, covering age 11-14 Years):**

This stage will comprise 3 years of education, building on the pedagogical & curricular style of the preparatory stage with the introduction of abstract concepts in each subject. Experiential learning within each subject and explorations of relations among different subject will be encouraged.

- **Secondary stage (Grades 9-12, covering ages 14-18):**

This stage will comprise of 4 years of multidisciplinary study, building on the subject- oriented pedagogical and curricular style of the middle stage with greater depth, Critical thinking, and attention of life aspirations, greater flexibility and student choice of subjects. In particular Students world continue to have the option of existing after grade 10 and re-entering in the next phase to pursue vocational or any other courses on grades 11-12, including at a more specialized school, if so desired.

Early Childhood Care Education(ECCE) framework:
Curricular framework for ECCE will be framed in the following way-

i. National Curricular and Pedagogical Framework for Early Childhood Education (NCPFECE) will be drafted by NCERT.

ii. NCPFECE will be aligned with the fastest research on ECCE, national & international best practices.

iii. A 3 month play-based "school preparation module" for all Grade 1 students to be developed by NCERT.

iv. Multi-faceted Framework- Comprising of alphabets, languages, numbers, counting, colours, shapes, indoor and outdoor play, puzzles and logical thinking, problem-solving, drawing, painting and other visual art, craft, drama and puppetry, music and movement

Learning in the formative years:
Learning items in the formative years are as follows:

i. Developing Curiosity,
ii. Logical thinking & Problem solving,
iii. Arts, Crafts & Music,
iv. Relationship with Nature,
v. Colours, Shapes, Alphabets & Numbers,
vi. Team work & Collaboration,
vii. Play-based & Discovery Based Learning,
viii. Ethics,
ix. Self-identity,
x. Etiquette, Behaviour and Emotional Development.

Foundational Literacy and Numeracy (FLN):
i. Early Learning:
The ability to read and write and perform basic operations is a necessary foundation and an indispensable pre-requisite for all future schooling and lifelong learning. As per survey reports made by various governmental and non-governmental organizations that approximately 5 crore students in elementary School have not attained foundational literacy and numeracy which indicates a learning crises.

ii. **National Mission:**

Attaining FLN for all children will thus become an urgent national mission with immediate measures to be taken on many fronts and with clear goals that will be attained in the short term. The highest priority of the education system will be to achieve universal FLN in primary school by

2025. To this end, a National Mission on FLN will be set up by MHRD on priority.

Studies around the world show one-on-one peer tutoring to be extremely effective for learning not just for the learner, but also for the tutor. Thus, peer tutoring can be taken up as a voluntary and joyful activity for fellow students under the supervision of trained teachers and by taking due care of safety aspects. Every literate member of the community could commit to teaching one student or person how to read, it would change the country's landscape very quickly.

iii. Availability of Trained Teacher:

First, teacher vacancies will be filled at the earliest especially in disadvantaged areas where illiteracy rate is high. Special attention will be given to employing local teachers who are familiar with local language. A pupil-teacher ratio will be 30: 1 or 25: 1 as per demand which will be ensured at the level of each school. Teachers will be trained, encouraged and supported with continuous professional development to impart FLN.

iv. Foundational Skills:

On the Curricular side, there will be an increased focus on foundational literacy and numeracy and generally, on reading, writing, speaking, counting arithmetic and mathematical thinking throughout the preparatory and middle school curriculum, with a robust system of continuous formative or adaptive assessment to track and thereby individualize and ensure each student's learning.

v. 3 month play based school:

Currently, with the lack of universal access to ECCE, a large proportion of children already fall behind within the first few weeks of Grade1. Thus, to ensure that all students are school ready, an interim 3 month play-based "School preparation module" for all Grade 1 students, consisting of activities and work books around the learning of alphabets, sounds words, colours, shapes, and numbers and involving collaborations with peers and parents, will be developed by NCERT and SCERTs.

vi. **National Repository:**

A National repository of high- quality resources on FLN will be made available on the Digital Infrastructure for Knowledge Sharing (DIKSHA). Technological interventions to serve as aids to teacher and to help bridge any language barriers that may exist between students and teachers, will be piloted and implemented.

vii. **Libraries:**

Enjoyable and inspirational books for student at all levels will be developed, including through high quality translation in all local and Indian Language, and will be made available extensively in both school and local public libraries. Digital libraries will able be established. School libraries will be set up particularly in villages to serve the community during non- school hours, and book clubs may meet in public or school libraries to further facilitate and propose widespread reading.

viii. **Book Promotion:**

A National Book promotion Policy will be formulated and extensive initiatives will be undertaken to ensure the availability, accessibility, quality and readership of books across geographics, languages and levels.
Reduction in Curriculum:

i. **Core Essentials:**

Curriculum in all subjects to be reduced to its core essentials.

ii. **Critical thinking:**

Focus on critical thinking, inquiry, discovery, discussion and analysis based teaching and learning methods for holistic education.

iii. **Interactive Classes:**

Interactive teaching with reduced dependency on text book learning; Questions from students will be promoted.

iv. **Experiential Learning:**

Fun, Creative, collaborative and exploratory activities in classroom for experiential learning and deeper student learning.
Teaching-Learning Strategies:

i. **Competency Based Education:**

Modules on preparing and implementing pedagogical plans based on competency and outcome based education for school leaders.

ii. **Integration of Subjects:**

Through arts integrated, sports integrated, ICT integrated and storytelling based pedagogy among others as standards pedagogy.

iii. **Development of Scientific Temper:**

Development of scientific temper and inculcation of knowledge and practice of human and constitutional values such as patriotism, sacrifice, non-violence, truth, honesty, peace etc.

iv. **No hard separation between**

a. Curricular or Co-Curricular or Extra- Curricular
b. Academic or Vocational
c. Science or humanities
d. Sports or art or academics

v. **Emphasis on Digital Literacy:**

Emphasis on digital literacy, coding and computational thinking, ethical and moral reasoning.

vi. **Promotion of Multi-Lingual Teaching:**

Promoting States to enter into bilateral agreements with nearly States to hire language teachers.

Mental and Physical health:

i. **Health Check up:**

Annual health check up for all students.

ii. **Reduce weight of school bags:**

Reduce weight of School bags and text books through suitable changes in curriculum & pedagogy.

iii. **Mandatory Skills:**

Mandatory skills to be imbibed by all students health, nutrition, physical education, fitness, wellness, sports, Besides training in preventive health care, mental health, first aid, personal and public hygiene will be included in the curriculum.

iv. **Hiring Counsellors:**

State governments will be encouraged to hire adequate no of counsellors & teachers.

v. **Focus on children with disability (CWD):**

Differentiated interventions and suitable infrastructure development at schools to make access easier for CWD.

vi. **Inclusive and Caring Culture at school:**

The role and expectations of Principal & teachers will explicitly include developing a caring & inclusive culture at School.
Innovative Pedagogy:

i. **Experiential Learning:**

Focus on experiential, inquiry and discovery based teaching learning methods.

ii. **Integrated Pedagogy:**

Emphasis on arts, sports & story –telling and ICT- integrated pedagogy.

iii. **Promotion of Peer tutoring:**

Promoting peer tutoring as voluntary and joyful activity under the supervision of teachers.

iv. **Equal Weightage:**

No hard separation between curricular, co-curricular & extra- curricular area. Freedom of choosing a variety of subject combination to be provided.

v. **Bagless days:**

Bagless days to be scheduled in academic calendar.

vi. **Use and Integration of technology:**

Integration of technology enabled pedagogy in classes 6-12.
Examination:

• **Grades 1 to 8:**

a. **Key stage assessments:** Censusassessments at key stage in classes 3, 5 and 8 to tract achievement.
b. **Achievement of critical learning outcomes:** Testing to focus on achievement of essential learning outcomes.
c. **Moving away from rote learning:** Assessment of Core concepts and knowledge, higher- order skills and its application in real life situations.
d. **Results of school examinations:**

The results of school examinations will be used only for developmental purposes and for continuous monitoring and improvement of the schooling system.

• **Grades 9-12:**

a. Board exams will be made 'easier' as they will test primarily core capacities or competencies.
b. Viable models to be explored: annual or semester or modular exams.
c. Two parts exams- objective type & descriptive type.
d. Guidelines will be prepared by NCERT, in consultation will SCERTs, Boards of Assessment (BoAS), and PARAKH.
e. Teachers to be prepared for a transformation in the assessment system by the 2022-23 academic session.
f. Each school board shall ensure equivalence of academic standards in learner's attainments

Multilingualism and the Power of Language Learning:

a. Medium of instruction up-to grade 5 and preferably till grade 8 and beyond, will be home language or mother-tongue or local language.
b. 'The Languages of India' a fun project or activity on to be taken by every student.
c. Three languages to be taught will be decided by State or UT.
d. All classical languages will be widely available in Schools as options.

Holistic Progress Card (PC):

i) States or UTs to redesign P.C in schools to make them holistic, 360 degree multidimensional report.

ii) P.C will include self-assessment, peer assessment & teacher-assessment.

iii. P.C to reflect the progress & uniqueness of learner in the cognitive, affective socio-emotional & psychomotor domains.
iv. Progress in project- based & inquiry based learning, quizzes, role plays, group work, port folios etc to be included in P.C.

v) The holistic P.C will actively involve parents in their children's education & development.

Development of Assessment Culture:

i)Continuous Tracking of learning outcomes of each child.

ii) Board Examinations to be more flexible, with assessment of essential skills.

iii) Assessment to focus on core concepts, higher order and foundational skills.

iv) Artificial Intelligence Based Software to help track the progress of the students to enable them to make optional career choices.

v. National Assessment Centre will help in bringing greater synergy in board examinations conducted by various Boards of Assessments.

vi. Self Assessment and Peer assessment

vii. The National Testing Agency (NTA) will work to offer a high- quality common aptitude test, to eliminate the need for taking coaching for these examinations.

Conclusion:

The key overall thrust of curriculum and pedagogy reform across all stages will be to move the education system towards real understanding and towards learning how to learn and away from the culture of role learning as is largely present today. The aim of education will not only be cognitive development, but also building character and creative holistic and well-rounded individuals equipped with the key 21st century skills. Curriculum frameworks & transaction mechanisms will be developed for ensuring that these skills and values are imbided through engaging processes of teaching and learning.

References:

- Bhura , Sneha (30 July 2020) . " In defence of M.Phill : Why the degree should not be discontinued . The Week . Retrieved 30 July 2020 .
- Free Entry – Exit Options Introduced For Students in NEP 2020 " . NDTV.com. Retrieved 21 september 2020 .
- Gohain , Manash Pratim (31 July 2020) . "NEP language policy broad guideline : Government " . The Times of India . Retrieved 31 July 2020.
- Kulkarni , Sagar (29 July 2020) " New policy offers 5-3-3-4 model of school education ". Deccan Herald . Retrieved 9 August 2020 .
- "National Education policy 2020 : Cabinet approves new national education policy : Key points " . The Times of India . 29 July 2020 .Retrieved 29 July 2020 .
- "National Education Policy: NTA to conduct common entrance exam for higher education institutes" .The Indian Express . 29 July 2020. Retrieved 30 July 2020.

- 4 – years Bed degree to be minimum qualification for teaching by 203 , says new NEP . Livemint. PTI . 30 July 2020 . Retrieved 31 July 2020.
- .Radhakrishnan , Akila (16 September 2020) . "Draft New Education Policy and Schools for the Skilling Age ".The Hindu Center . Retrieved 31 July 2020.
- Vishnoi ,Anubhuti (31 July 2020) . " No switch in instruction medium from English to regional languages with NEP'20 : HRD " . The Economic Times . Retrieved 31 July 2020 .

CHAPTER XV

Curriculum Reforms In India- National Curriculum Framework (NCF) 2020

Mr. UdayModak,*Mr.Suman Gupta

• • •

Introduction

A process of **curriculum** change in higher education institutions, involving an interplay of global, national and institutional factors. Generally takes many forms and directions within which the meanings and methods of education delivery are altered.Curriculum reform is the process of making changes to the curriculum with the intent of making learning and teaching more meaningful and effective.Curriculum reform is necessary for every and single country because it provide meaningful and effective knowledge.

The NEP 2020 may include adolescent education program and national population education program, educational technology like computational thinking from age six onwards and vocational education in the school curriculum. This NEP will be framed after 15 years of gap. The HRD Ministry along with NCERT is working on the selection of the chairperson for the committee.

Definitions of Curriculum and Reform:

Reform is easier to define than curriculum. Reform merely meansto reshape, to reconfigure, to make different. But mere change does notmean improvement. So, too, with reform; thus, the saga of re-form thatwe review here is not intended to imply an evolutionary development.Reformers themselves generally hope that their brand of reform willbring improvement; it is their inspiration to pursue their cause. Therefore, as we think about the past fifty years of curriculum reform, weneed to ask whether the re-forming carried out was improvement ornot.The term curriculum is shrouded in definitional controversy, somuch so that it would require a book-length treatment to begin to dealwith it. For our discussion, curriculum means whatever is advocated for teaching and learning. This includes both schooland non-school environments; both overt and hidden curriculums; andbroad as well as narrow notions of content—its development, acquisition, and consequences.

Curriculum Development Technologies:

The term technology refers here to systematic treatment, not the kind of hardware used in curriculum development for reform. Thus, a popular approach, such as strategic planning, is a form of technology. The intellectual traditionalist would be less supportive than the others of placing great emphasis on curriculum development, claiming that the curriculum (the classics and knowledge disciplines) are already developed. It is merely a matter of providing students with what is known. In great contrast, the social behaviourist calls for a detailed needs analysis as a basis for forming purposes, followed by in-depth analysis as purposes are translated into manageable behavioural objectives. Behaviourists systematically delineate learning activities that serve as vehicles for the objectives; design the route (scope, sequence, environment, and instructional models) through which the objectives and activities take shape; and evaluate how well the objectives are realized. The evaluation of the process then guides revision and shapes the next curriculum reform. For the experientialist, the steps of curriculum development appear to be much less systematic; yet, structure is there but more deeply embedded in the fabric of human interaction. Rather than a top-down orientation to curriculum development (i.e., planning by experts, to be distributed to teachers and learners), curriculum development is seen as a natural function of school and classroom life. The structure or systematic treatment (technology) of curriculum development is evolutionary—formed through communication in small groups who work on projects that evolve into other projects in a continuing sequence. The conciliator admits that such "natural" curriculum development can sometimes occur when certain kinds of ideal teachers and students meet. On the other hand, the conciliarist tends to lean heavily on more overtly structured forms of curriculum development. The conciliator encourages input from teachers, learners, parents, and relevant others, but usually stops short of giving these groups full reign in actually creating the curriculum.

Objectives:

The major objectives are as follows:

1. The study will Promote and co-ordinate research in all the branches of curriculum.
2. The study will Improve new trends and techniques in school curriculum.

3. The study will Undertake studies, investigations and surveys relating to school curriculum.
4. The study will Maintain close contact with similar national and international bodies.

Key Versions Of The Indian Curriculum:

There are two key versions of the Indian curriculum: the CBSE (Central Board of Secondary Education) and the CISCE (Council for the Indian School Certificate Examinations). Our international schools offer both of these pathways to our students. There are a few differences between the two schemes which are worth noting:

- The CBSE curriculum is designed and developed by the National Council of Educational Research and Training, New Delhi. It prepares students for the All India CBSE Secondary Schools Examination at age 16 (end of grade 10) and the All India Senior School Certificate Examination at age 18 (end of grade 12).
- The CISCE curriculum prepares students for the ISCE examination in secondary school and the ISC (Indian School Certificate) examination in the final year of secondary school.

Why choose the Indian curriculum?

At our Indian curriculum schools both overseas and in India, students benefit from a highly supportive system which encourages them to strive to reach their full, individual potential. Both of the Indian curricula we offer give students of all abilities and aptitudes the chance to achieve their very best in a broad range of subjects including:

- Business studies
- Information technology
- Indian languages
- Maths, English & the sciences
- The arts

The CBSE and the CISCE open exciting doors for GEMS students. Indian universities are closely interlinked with these secondary school systems. This means that successful students have a golden ticket to India's best higher education establishments.

The Indian curriculum is also rapidly gaining recognition and respect worldwide. We're very proud of our students from GEMS Indian curriculum schools, many of whom have been extremely successful in qualifying for places at prestigious international universities.

Focus: culture & opportunity:

Our Indian curriculum schools celebrate Indian culture and values. Teachers and families share a common belief that a good education is a passport to life's opportunities.

Key features:

i.   Highly respected national and regional systems
v.   Strong focus on academics
v.   Covers wide ability range
v.   Tried and tested
v.   Recently revised
v.   Growing acceptance for university entrance worldwide

Need for Curriculum Reforms:

- To restructure the curriculum according to the needs of learners society.
- To eliminate the necessary units, teaching method and content.
- To introduce latest and update method of teaching and content , new knowledge and practices.
- There is too much emphasize on the subject matter.

Factors Influencing The Curriculum Reforms:

1. **Staffing Issues:**

Including workload, we have committed on financial matters, and the effect they can have on curriculum activities.

2.Students Abilities

In an ideal world, our program would be dictated by our desire to create graduates of the highest possible calibre. And,were we capable of sourcing the correct raw material in sufficient quantity, perhaps we could achieve that goal.

3. **Financial Pressures**

Clearlythere are powerful budgetary forces that influences our decisions.

4.Influential Individuals

Strong leadership accepted by the academic staff ,that have a capacity to attract other academic staff to rally behind principled educational objectives that are supported within the environment.

5. University And Government Regulations:

University administration increasingly push the case for efficient use of resources. While the number of programs offered in our disciplines has beengrowingfor a long time, and the closing down of programs is uncommon. There is usually considerable pressure to discontinue to low-enrolmentsubjects.

Major Reformsof National Education Policy2020:

The recent National Education Policy (NEP) 2020 in India comes 34 years after the previous policy, announced in 1986 and revised in 1992. It took six years of work and consultations with thousands of educators, policymakers, and members of civil society. It was truly a democratic effort and is highly aspirational, aiming for India to "have an education system by 2040, that is second to none, with equitable access to the highest quality education for all learners, regardless of social and economic background."

The NEP's chief purpose is to reform the education system and bridge the gap between current learning outcomes and those desired. Recognizing the need to keep up with a rapidly changing world and knowledge landscape, the NEP 2020 articulates that "[t]he purpose of the education system is to develop good human beings capable of rational thought and action, possessing compassion and empathy, courage and resilience, scientific temper and creative imagination, with sound ethical moorings and values. It aims at producing engaged, productive, and contributing citizens for building an equitable, inclusive and plural society as envisaged by our constitution."

Such strong emphasis on equity and quality is laudable, as is the effort to broaden the scope of "quality education." The policy proposes a move away from content-heavy curricula in order "to make space for critical thinking, more holistic, inquiry-based, discovery-based, discussion-based and analysis-based learning." Giving equal importance to co-curricular activities (i.e., arts, sports, vocational skills), it mandates a shift toward multidisciplinary education, away from rigid silos of "arts," "science," and "commerce" streams, with renewed focus on 21ˢᵗ century skills. This is a welcome breath of fresh air, given that the current system is strongly driven by rote learning and content-based examinations, divorced from any real application to life.

Below are the most notable points of reform proposed by the NEP 2020:

1. *Inclusion of early childhood education*: Education will begin at age 3, rather than at age 6 for students in first grade, to focus on children's foundational years (ages 3-8). Previously, children's right to education applied to grades one through eight (6-14 years); the NEP aims to extend this right to children ages 3-18. This is particularly relevant for public schools, which serve a majority of children from low-income families and who, compared to middle-class families, often lack preschool education, thereby widening the gap between them further.

2. *A focus on equity and inclusion:* An entire section is devoted to the inclusion of Socio-Economically Disadvantaged Groups (SEDGs), broadly categorized as girls, transgender and children with special needs, children from rural areas, Dalits, and victims of trafficking. Additionally, it recognizes that children with disabilities are not receiving the attention required to learn and thrive in schools, primarily because teachers are simply not trained or equipped to address their learning needs. Thus, it makes an effort to ensure teachers are adequately prepared in the area of special education. Lastly, the NEP recognizes that children in SEDGs are those who most frequently are unenrolled, drop out, and learn less and "recommends that the policies and schemes designed to include students in SEDGs ... should be especially targeted towards girls."

3. *An expanded concept of "quality":* Given the poor basic literacy and numeracy outcomes reported, the new NEP aims to create a solid foundation for children during their early development by establishing a National Mission on Foundational Literacy and Numeracy that would prioritize "the development of communication and early language, literacy and numeracy." The NEP also calls for much-needed teacher education reform, including an overhaul of pre-service programs, including the B.Ed, and for the first time, mental health and social-emotional learning receive a strong mention. The need to leverage technology is also recognized, along with intentions to extend optical

fibers to the remotest villages and achieve universal digital access and literacy.

The NEP 2020 is ambitious and progressive, as was the NEP 1986 and the Right to Education Act 2009. There is an enormous opportunity for India's considerable young population to become its biggest strength. However, to achieve this, the government must fully commit itself to the policy's implementation with the political will and urgency it deserves.

While the document takes great strides in advocating a more inclusive and equitable system, especially for girls, it does not go far enough. "Gender sensitivity" is mentioned repeatedly throughout the document, but it does not address the need for systemic change. Strong patriarchal social and political structures—and their inherent discrimination and violence against women—must be questioned, critiqued, and recognized as contradictory to India's constitutional values of equality. The same is true of castes: Though the NEP recommends special efforts to help castes access and remain in schools as SEDGs, there is no mention of caste prejudice, nor of the need to work toward its eradication. Teacher training programs and school curricula should include a focus on eradicating a discriminatory caste consciousness and hierarchical caste identities. Similarly, education focused on gender power dynamics should be compulsory in school curricula in order to develop egalitarian mind-setin boys and girls from a young age, including in early childhood education. This is imperative if we are to change the "social customs and mores," as the policy euphemistically refers to the discriminatory social structures.

Given the enormity of India's school system (1,522,346 schools, 8,691,922 teachers, and 260 million students) and the country's regional, linguistic, and cultural diversity, universalizing quality education is a challenge; yet, the policy says little on the issue of governance and management. Robust systems for managing the large public school system have yet to be developed, and governance represents the government's greatest challenge. Data collection, monitoring, and accountability systems are weak and inadequate. Without the strong, efficient governance of a well-functioning public school system, the reforms outlined above will fail.

Furthermore, serious political commitment must be demonstrated, including adequate budgetary allocation, personnel training, and improved curriculum development and infrastructure. While the NEP commits to increasing the education budget from its current 4-6 percent of the GDP, this was also promised earlier but never materialized. Additionally (and more importantly), efficient and judicious marshalling and management of *all* available resources is needed, including in the private sector.

Similar to the policy's development, a democratic approach should be followed during the NEP's implementation. The Uttar Pradesh state government has solicited recommendations from civil society organizations, and I recommend it go one step further by partnering actively with civil society organizations, private foundations, the corporate sector, private schools, and communities. To improve both access to and quality of education, particularly in the pubic school system, the government should harness innovative solutions, including through the use of technology, developed by several NGOs.

Education is a public good. Everyone is a stakeholder and should therefore be invited to contribute to actualize the vision of the NEP to make India's education system strong, inclusive, and equitable.

Conclusion:

Curricular reform, be it of an entire school curriculum or a significant longitudinal component shouldfollow as much as possible the current wisdom of educational innovation and change strategy. It should follow aclear vision and mission, a selected educational paradigm,and pay attention to stakeholders, context, culture andpolitics. It goes beyond the technical and is complex. Assuch, a strong leadership support and early winsare paramount. The design should allow for the emergenceof unintended consequences. Implementation needs careful planning and monitoring and the evaluation should bemulti-faceted, employing a mixed-method innovative design with short- and long-term components.

References:

- https://www.gemseducation.com/choosing-a-school/which-curriculum/indian-curriculum/
- **Sahni, Urvashi (Friday, October 2, 2020)** India's National Education Policy 2020: A reformist step forward?
- **Sreetha Akhil (June 5,2019)ppt.** curriculum change, curriculum model, curriculum model, published by education.
- **Schubert, W.H.(1986).** Curriculum: perspective, paradigm and possibilities.
- **Schubert, W.H. (1991).** Historical perspective on centralizing curriculum.

CHAPTER XVI

Curriculum development concept and principle

**Dr. Mukta Goyal, ***Swati Singh

• • •

Introduction

What is curriculum development?

The manner in which we comprehend and guess educational programs today has changed fundamentally throughout the long term. Today, the most straightforward meaning of "educational program" is the subjects that make up a course of study at schools, colleges or universities. The word educational program has been established in Latin. It initially signified "hustling chariot" and came from the action word currere, "to run." Curriculum advancement is inseparable from course arranging or course improvement.

Perceive that distinction in course configuration exist: a numerical course taken at one college may cover similar material, yet the instructor may show it in an alternate manner. Be that as it may, the center essentials of educational program advancement continue as before.

What are the different categories of curriculum development?

Current educational program can be stalled into two general classifications: the item class and the interaction classification. The item class is results-situated. Grades are the superb target, with the emphasis lying more on the completed item as opposed to on the learning cycle. The interaction class, nonetheless, is more open-finished, and centers around how learning creates throughout some stretch of time. These two classifications should be considered when creating educational program.

Principles of curriculum development

(a) Suitability to the age and mental level of the kids

What is to be given to the kids through learning encounters at a specific age and grade level should suit their age and mental turn of events

The limit with regards to seeing, how kids develop with age. The substance of the examination in any subject ought to be framed to suit their psychological capacity.

(b) According to the particular interests of understudies

Youngsters will actually want to learn better in fields where they have uncommon preferences and tendency of the brain. It is likewise discovered that at various phases old enough gatherings, youngsters have distinctive interest designs.

Interests of kids additionally change as indicated by conditions and circumstances.

Consequently learning encounters ought to be intended to suit the interests and tastes of the age gathering of understudies.

(c) The educational plan ought to be ecologically focused

The substance of the learning encounters for kids ought to be connected with the requirements of the climate wherein they live.

For instance, kids from rustic regions can comprehend and get a handle on effectively the data which is straightforwardly worried about their encounters in their own provincial climate.

Exactly the same thing applies to youngsters in different conditions like metropolitan regions, uneven regions, and so forth

(d) The guideline of the far-reaching educational program

The educational program should have the vital subtleties. Rundown of themes to be covered doesn't settle the reason.

The two educators and understudies should know obviously what is generally anticipated of them, what is the start and what is the finish of the subject for the specific class. Material, guides, exercises, life circumstances and so on ought to be recorded in the educational program.

(e) Principle of co-connection

The educational program ought to be to such an extent that every one of the subjects are related with one another.

While planning the educational program, it should be remembered that the topic of different subjects has some connection to one another so they help the kid in the end.

(f) The rule of functional work

Youngsters are dynamic ordinarily. They like new things and can learn more by doing or by action technique. Hence educational program ought to be planned so that it gives greatest freedom to the youngster for functional work with the assistance of substantial things.

(g) Principle of adaptability

Rather than being inflexible educational program should give the indication of adaptability.

The association of the educational plan ought to be based on singular contrasts as each youngster is unique in relation to the next.

Aside from these states of society continue evolving, accordingly, the educational plan should be adequately adaptable to address the necessities as goals of the general public.

(h) Principle of forward-looking

This standard requests the consideration of those subjects, content and learning encounters that may demonstrate accommodating to the understudies in driving their future life in an appropriate way.

(I) The standard of discussion with instructors

Instructors assume a critical part in the execution of the school educational program of any grade or stage.

It is accordingly very fundamental for look for the appropriate association of the educators in the development and advancement of the school educational program.

(j) The standard of the joint endeavor

It's anything but a joint endeavor where different specialists are included like instructive analysts, instructive technologists, educational program trained professionals, assessment trained professionals, instructors, topic specialists and so on.

(k) The guideline of accessibility of time and different assets

Educational program is the way to understand the results of the instructive destinations of the school. Execution of the educational plan is similarly significant as educational program development. While creating educational program specialists ought to likewise remember its execution. They ought to know about the states of the schools and conceivable accessibility of time and assets accessible.

Need and importance of curriculum development (or construction)

IMPORTANCE OF CURRICULUM DEVELOPMENT

- Curriculum Development has a broad scope because it is not only about the school, the learners and the teachers,
- It is also provides answers or solution to the world's pressing condition and problems, such as environment, politics, socio economic, and other issues of poverty, climate changes and sustainable development
- There must be a chain of developmental process to develop a society , First, the school curriculum , particularly in higher education, must be developed to preserve the country's national identity and to ensure its economy's growth and stability

slideshare

- Educational program improvement is an intentional action.
- It is embraced to plan or overhaul for the acknowledgment of certain particular instructive targets.
- The educational program is the core of the understudy's school/school insight.
- The educational plan ought to be evaluated and updated consistently with the goal that it can serve the changing requirements of the two understudies and society.
- The accompanying focuses emphasize the requirements and significance of educational plan improvement.

1. **Clear reason and objectives:-** Curriculum development give composed curricular objectives which are only proposed understudy advancement results. These objectives and targets are indicated in extensive detail and in social language.
2. **Persistent appraisal and improvement of value:-** Valid and solid evaluation of the educational plan is vital. The educational program followed by an establishment ought to be explored routinely to keep up with it's adequacy concerning the changing necessities of the general public overall.
3. **A judicious arrangement:-** In an educational plan instructive exercises are painstakingly requested in a formative grouping. This formative arrangement assists with framing a very much arranged (or

coherent)curriculum dependent on expected objectives and results of the educational plan and its constituent courses.

4. **Making system in educating and learning:-** Curriculum advancement helps in proposing reasonable educating learning methodologies, showing techniques, informative materials, and so on It helps in accommodating the legitimate execution of the educational plan with respect to instructors and students

5. **. Helps in the determination of learning encounters:-** Curriculum improvement is required for proper choice and association of learning encounters. It helps in the determination of study matter and different exercises so students can gain objectives and goals of instructing.

Educational plan improvement considers the need of giving a plan of schooling to CCE of the instructing learning results. With appropriate criticism, it assists with acquiring fundamental improvement the instructing learning cycle and climate.

Conclusion

A formative way to deal with the educational programs getting ready for MH youngsters is considered attractive. The educational program content ought to be useful, targeting advancing the overall advancement of these kids and assisting them with having an autonomous existence and incorporate into the local area.

References:

- https://simplyeducate.me/2014/12/13/the-meaning-and-importance-of-curriculum-development/
- http://uafulucknow.ac.in/wp-content/uploads/2020/03/CURRICULUM-DEVELOPMENT-MA-education-2nd-sem.pdf
- http://www.vkmaheshwari.com/WP/?p=1833
- http://egyankosh.ac.in/bitstream/123456789/42010/1/Unit-1.pdf
- https://www.academia.edu/35768464/The_Concept_of_Curriculum_and_
- Curriculum_Development_Curriculum_and_Material_Development_The_
- Definition_of_Curriculum
- https://tophat.com/blog/curriculum-development-models-design/
- https://physicscatalyst.com/graduation/principles-of-curriculum-development/

- https://www.slinger.k12.wi.us/district/Policies/mixed_policies/330.doc
- https://physicscatalyst.com/graduation/curriculum-development-need-importance/

CHAPTER XVII

Teacher Empowerment Through Management And Approaches Of Curriculum

**Dr. Kotra Balayogi

• • •

Abstract

Education is the process of development, in which efforts are made for the all-around development of any child, it involves the processes teaching, training, instruction, etc. The learning experiences are provided with the help of the activities for bringing desirable behavioural change among students and the learning situations are generated by teaching tasks in which student gains new experiences, understanding, knowledge, etc. which is the aims and objective of teaching and learning process. An outline of the content in the narrow sense is known as curriculum or syllabus and the teaching structure is based on a format of curriculum, which is the pivot of any context of education. The present study focuses on the curriculum which is based on the social philosophy and changing according to needs of the society as well as nation, and attempts on the management of the curriculum and its approaches, which is very crucial for the syllabus for any course in the modern education. Therefore, the study is dedicated to management and various approaches towards curriculum development as a source of relevant, timely and comprehensive knowledge management in all types of 21st century educational institutions in India.

Keywords: curriculum, management, development, approaches, teaching, teacher's role

Introduction

An old concept of curriculum was to consider it is merely syllabus or an outline of courses to study. The curriculum word is of Latin language. It means 'race course'. In education it means 'work field of student' or race course of the students. It consists of two words-race and course. The word 'course' means curriculum and race refers students' experiences and activities. A teacher performs his teaching activities in view of curriculum.

The new concept of curriculum is very broad based. It consists 'he totality of experiences that a pupil receives through the ᵐanifold activities that go on in the school, in a classroom, library, 'aboratory, workshop and play-ground and in the numerous contacts between the teachers and the pupils. It is neither dogmatic nor rigid in its form and structure. It is neither uniform nor standardised to conform to a prescribed pattern. It is characterized by variety and flexibility and is tailored to the needs of the students at different age levels. It gives the students an increasing awareness of the around them so that they may fit in more efficiently in the milieu of community life. It thus secures more integrated group relations, The Secondary Education Commission has also pointed out clearly the nature and Conception of the desired curriculum: "It must be clearly understood that, according to the best, educational thought, curriculum does not mean only the academic subject traditionally taught in the school but it includes the totality of experience that child receives at school. In this sense, the whole life of the school becomes the curriculum which can touch the life of the students at all points and help in the development o/a balanced personality."

The term 'Curriculum has been defined by the scholars and educationists. Cunninghum says that. "It (curriculum) is a tool in the hands of the artist (teacher) to mould his material (pupil) according to his ideal (objective) in his studio (school). " Frobel says that, "Curriculum should be conceived as an epitome of the rounded whole of the knowledge and experience of the human race." According to Taylor "The curriculum consists of content and teaching methods and purpose may be in its rough form and 'nay have a sufficient definition which is to start with."

Curriculum Management

The term curriculum development is most popular while Management of Curriculum is very recent concept introduced in education and I.K. Devies has used the term managing teaching and learning and teacher is a manager, his approach has initiated and introduced the term 'Management' in education process and the term management has been defined by the experts of other disciplines e.g., industry, business, politics, etc. It refers to conscious preference from variety of alternative plus proposals and further the more that such choices involve purpose full commitment to recognise and derived objectives and it employs strategies to achieve the all types of educational objectives.

Approaches towards Curriculum Teaching

Herbert Approach

Focus: The teaching at memory level aims at causing learning that may enable the student:

1. To train the mental discipline
2. To acquire factual information
3. To retain the learnt material for longer time
4. To recall and recognise the learned material

Syntax: The structure of the model is developed with help of following formal steps:

- Preparation: The function of this step is to bring into consciousness relevant ideas of the subject-matter and the teacher plans about the presentation of the content.
- Presentation: The new ideas/knowledge of content is imparted in such a way that it may be linked with earlier knowledge of the students.
- Comparison and Abstraction: In this step, the teacher attempts to compare between new system, new facts and new ideas to identify similarities among new facts.
- Generalisation: In this step teacher generates the situations so that students are able to point out similarities if elements of new ideas and knowledge.
- Application: Teacher creates situations/problems so that student may use memorised facts for the further facts and the mathematical tables are used in multiplication and division.

Social System: This model consists of authoritarian behaviour and the teacher is more active and his/her main job is to structure and to present the content systematically and logically in the class.

The learner is like a passive listener in classroom. The social system is such that teacher can teach even wrong things to students at this level, the form of motivation is purely extrinsic and the teacher motivation through reward verbal praise and punishment. It the learner motivated or reinforced continuously then he learns better.

Support System: This model requires some supportive devices co make it more effective and more meaningful material should be used to present at level and the subject matter should be made definite in its structure.

Evaluation System: The evaluation is an indispensable aspect of teaching because it produces evidences about the realisation of goals of the teaching model. Usually, oral tests are given to measure the retention of learned material and the objective test of recall and recognition type are administered to evaluate the knowledge of students.

Morrison Approach

- **Focus:** The main focus of understanding level teaching is to have the mastery over the concept this model is idea-centred. It provides substantial knowledge to subject matter and to encourage adaptive responses in the memory level teaching for achieving these objectives.
- **Syntax:** The structure of understanding level teaching involves the following steps:
- **Exploration:** It consists of three operations, it involves testing, questioning to explore initial learning of the students, it provides apperceptive sequences, where he should start and it intends to assist teacher to arrange subject matter in psychological sequence.
- **Presentation:** It includes three activities and teacher presents the new content into small units and he/she attempts to maintain continuous rapport with the students in the class and the teacher tests the students to diagnose/observes how many students fail to grasp the presented content. It is necessary that the presentation is repeated, teacher should not proceed towards the new unit until most of the students fully understand. **Assimilation:** At the end of presentation a test is administered, when students have passed out the test of presentation and teacher moves to assimilation. The purpose of assimilation is thoroughness of subject matter and the students are active in this step they do much work in library, laboratory, field work, assignments and to consult source material. A mastery test is also administered at the end of assimilation and if students can't pass the test, they are asked for further assimilation.
- **Organisation:** An organisation provides an apperceptive sequence and when student passes a mastery test and thus terminates a period of assimilation and moves towards the organisation step. It involves the following operations like organisation's step is to determine whether he can reproduce the essentials of the unit in writing without any help. This step is especially essential in subjects of extensive content which include a large number of elements in one learning unit.

- **Recitation:** A student can move up to the last step directly from assimilation in certain subjects and also, when the period of organisation and terminates and each student presents orally before the teacher, his/her classmates in a condensed version of the understanding taught in the unit.
- **Social System:** Teachers should be active enough to see that he/she should not be authoritarian and he/she should be democratic in teaching in the classroom. He/she has to act as a leader of the group and his/her main job is to guide and to motivate the students. His/her efforts should be of discovering and mastering the truth and his/her behaviour should be flexible, dynamic and full of human touch.
- **Support System:** This System is helpful to make this model effective and goals may be achieved and the teaching aids should be more presentation stage so that it may not be repeated several times. The audio-visual aids and other devices may be used for an effective presentation and this system is much various more useful sources at assimilation stage. The teacher's proper supervision is very essential at the stage of assimilation and the learners should be given an opportunity to practice the learnt material according to their own.

Evaluation Approach

The concept of evaluation approach is given by B.S. Bloom and his main emphasis was that testing should be based on teaching and both these activities should be objective-centred. Today teaching is organised by using the evaluation approach. Under this approach yearly plan and unit plan are prepared and the education process is considered as tri-polar process. In this the fundamental elements are education objectives, learning experiences, and change of behaviour of evaluation approach. The evaluation approach and educational process are closely related to each other and the effectiveness and appropriateness of educational process is ascertained by evaluation approach. The evaluation approach is a new concept in the discipline of education, which has revolutionized the process of education, in this approach main emphasis has been given in realising the objectives of education in behavioural terms. Quillen and Hima have defined the term evaluation approach as "evaluation is the process of gathering and interpreting evidences on changes in the behaviour of the students as they progress through school." In evaluation approach teaching and testing activities are performed side by side and the term evaluation is used in broader sense and it does not confine only up to student achievement but it includes the total process of teaching and learning.

B. S. Bloom Steps in Evaluation Approach

B. S. BLOOM STEPS IN EVALUATION APPROACH

1. Educational Objectives (E.O.)

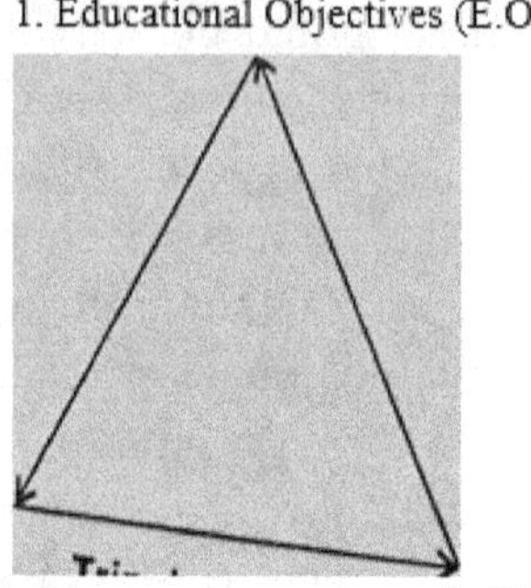

2. Learning Experience (L.E.)   3. Change of Behaviour (C.B.)

TRIPOLAR PROCESS

These three steps are closely related to each other and are performed in a sequence and the teaching and testing activities go side by side and these are objective-centred. The main assumption of this approach is that failure of the student is due to the inappropriateness of learning experiences of teaching, because it is main responsibility of teacher to bring desirable change among students and thus, the change of behaviour and evaluations in terms of the school subject which are taught to them for providing learning experiences.

Management Approach of Curriculum

The concept of teaching, levels of teaching models of teaching and learning, strategies of teaching provide theoretical knowledge of teaching to teachers and pupil-teachers. But this awareness of teaching does not orient the pupil teachers how to plan and organise their teaching and about managing teaching-learning. This knowledge and understanding are very essential during the training period of the understanding and skill for managing teaching-learning process effectively. The training institutions are providing knowledge about Herbartian steps of teaching that is preparation and presentation. Herbartian approach of teaching gives too much emphasis on presentation but it does not focus on the purpose and goals of teaching while teaching is considered as purposeful activity and the teaching is organised to achieve some specific goals of education. Now, the present approach of teaching gives main emphasis on objectives. I.K. Davies considers that teaching is a noble profession. He has given a new concept managing teaching-learning' in the field of education. The concept the practical steps for planning and organising teaching activities in classroom situation and the pupil and teacher can make use of these steps in organising his classroom teaching. Davies has borrowed this concept of managing teaching-learning from other human organisations.

Integrated Approach of Curriculum

The experiments were conducted in psychology in the beginning of 20th century. Gestalt psychology was also introduced and it was proved that mind is a unit and mind receive the knowledge as whole not in parts, whole knowledge is stable in the mind. These researches and inventions have also influenced education and an integrated curriculum was introduced in U.S.A. This type of curriculum is based on the unification theory. The ideas and activities will be useful only when these can combine in a unit and the project-method is used in an integrated curriculum and it is an activity-centred curriculum. Group-controlled instruction are employed in this type of curriculum and it is also known as an activity-oriented curriculum. The knowledge of all subject is imparted by relating to some social activity and the activity should be related to life and the main focus is to develop social efficiency among the students. There is no compartment of subject and the knowledge is considered as a unit. The subject content are the parts of an activity. An activity is assigned to a group of students, the required knowledge of the subjects for performing the activity are given to the students and the learning by doing technique is used in this type of curriculum. The school subjects are integrated and correlated and the courses of study should be related to real life situations. According to Henderson, there should not be any barrier or compartmentalization among the subject and it provides such experiences to the students which is easy to understand and easy to use. The approach is given by pragmatic philosophy and Kilpartic has employed the project-method and introducing integrated approach to curriculum and it employs group- controlled instruction which must be activity-oriented method of instruction.

Conclusion and Implications

The curriculum is clear about what has to be taught and what should be learned at each stage of schooling, is based on reasonable expectations of time and resources, and is flexible and developed collaboratively with schools and jurisdictions (Australian Curriculum, Assessment and Reporting Authority, 2010a). Curriculum is the foundation of the teaching and learning process and it involves developing programs of study, teaching strategies, resources allocations, specific lesson plans and assessment of students, and faculty development (Alberta Education, 2012). Approaches to management of curriculum in higher education institutions is a prime concern for all stakeholders, educators, policy-makers, government, parents and the society at large (Alberta Education, 2012; De Coninck, 2008). Educational institutions and employers alike are of the view that education should help students gain knowledge and basic skills (Bounds, 2009). Designing appropriate curriculum is crucial for providing such knowledge and skills moreover, there is a growing need for higher education institutions to respond to the changing environment in a positive and learner-centered manner through quality curriculum. Students who have learned to adapt to change and to adapt their abilities to a variety of contexts and situations, develop managerial competencies for a turbulent world (Pacheco, 2000, cited in Bounds, 2009). Interestingly the theory and practice of curriculum management in educational institutions have remained and continue to be hotly debated themes in academia, mainly because there are different definitions and interpretations of the term curriculum in addition to variations in approaches to curriculum design. Most importantly, the terms "curriculum" and "education" though defined and interpreted differently in theory, nonetheless, are interrelated and inseparable in practice. Curriculum is critical in providing high-quality educational programs and services; however, there are gaps between how curriculum is developed and how curriculum is supposed to be managed in theory and it is considered as a foundation stone for the well-being and effectiveness of higher education (Barnett & Coate, 2005, p. 7). The present study provides a theoretical-conceptual framework that could be used for defining the approaches of curriculum management that is development, implementation, evaluation, etc. by all stakeholders in all types of educational institutions in India. The teaching objectives are achieved objectives by providing learning experiences to the students and the learning experiences are controlled by teaching objectives and textbooks of the subject. Teaching can be main effective by creating appropriate learning experiences and these experiences should provide the appropriate learning experiences. A teacher role is to organise and control all the teaching activities and a teacher has to organise and create learning situations for providing experiences to the students according to their available resources. Teachers should behave to the students like philosophers, instructors and friends and the learning experiences vary subject to subject. A teacher has also to plan about the evaluative techniques for ascertaining the teaching objectives and in the presentation of teaching content and preparing test for evaluation purpose, a teacher has to consider the needs and level of students in view of his teaching content. Future studies on curriculum management can be carried out involving interested educational institutions in order to see their practices including designing, implementation, evaluation process, etc. of curriculum towards a focus on the learning objectives and learning outcomes intended in the curriculum and the actual achievement of these critical ingredients of any curriculum at educational level in the 21st century.

References

Alberta Education. (2012). Curriculum development processes, from knowledge to action. Retrieved from http://www.education.alberta.ca/media/6809242/d_chapter1.pdf

Australian Curriculum, Assessment and Reporting Authority. (2010a). The shape of the Australian curriculum, version 2.0. Retrieved from http://www.acara.edu.au/verve/_resources/Shape_of_the_Australian_Curriculum.pdf

Carl, A. E. (2009). Teacher empowerment through curriculum development: Theory into practice (3rd ed.). Juta and Company Ltd., SA.

Egan, K. (1979). Educational development. New York: Oxford University Press.

Huba, M. E., & Freed, J. E. (2000). Learner-centered assessment on college campuses: Shifting the focus from teaching to learning. Needham Heights, MA: Alleyn and Bacon.

Krull, E., & Kurm, H. (1996). Hilda Taba—A worldwide known educator from Estonia: Taba's biography, ideas, and impact on Estonian education. Retrieved from www.schulmuseum.at/publikationen/retrospektiven.doc

Ornstein A. C., & Hunkins, F. P. (2009). Curriculum foundations, principles and issues (5th ed.). Boston: Allyn and Bacon.

Taba, H. (1962). Curriculum development—Theory and practice. New York.

Tyler, R. W. (1969). Basic principles of curriculum and instruction (2nd ed.). Chicago, IL: University of Chicago Press. http://dx.doi.org/10.7208/chicago/9780226820323.001.0001

CHAPTER XVIII

Curriculum Development: Perspectives, Principles And Issues

Krittibas Datta,* Pranati Das

• • •

Introduction:

The process by which an instructor or institution produces or accepts a course plan is known as curriculum development. Because this is such a vast topic, it can be tough to cut through the clutter to identify current best practises. There are also numerous schools of thought on how to effectively approach the process of curriculum development.

According to modern thinking, education is a tri-polar process in which the instructor is on one end, the student is on the other, and the curriculum is on the third. In fact, the curriculum is the axis around which the educational process revolves. If education is defined as the process of teaching and learning, then only the curriculum is used to teach and learn. In this light, we might say that education is intertwined with our lives.

The word "curriculum" comes from the Latin word "currere," which meaning "racing course." As a result, the term "curriculum" connotes a sense of rivalry and goal attainment.

The curriculum encompasses the entire environment. Those who define curriculum as including the entire educational environment provide the most comprehensive definition. "The curriculum is all that goes on in the lives of the children, their parents, and their teachers," writes H.L. Caswell. Everything that surrounds the learner during his working hours is included in the curriculum." The curriculum has been dubbed "the environment in action" by some. In today's world, the term is used in a more liberal sense because there is no denying that a child's education is influenced by a variety of factors, including books, the playground, library, laboratory, reading room, extra-curricular programmes, the educational environment, and a variety of other factors.

Principles of Curriculum Development

Different educators have voiced their opinions on the essential principles of curriculum development, with the differences stemming from their differing educational philosophies. The following are the basic principles of curriculum development in a nutshell:

Principle utility: -

The educationist T.P. Nunn believes that the most fundamental factor behind the creation of a curriculum is utility. "While the common man loves his children to pick up some pieces of useless learning for merely aesthetic purposes," he adds, "he requires, on the whole, that they be taught what will be helpful to them in later life, and he is disposed to give 'useful' a very tight meaning." In general, parents support including all subjects in the curriculum that are likely to be useful to their child throughout his life and that will enable him to become a responsible member of society.

Principle of training in the proper patterns of conduct: -

The basic premise underpinning the development of a curriculum, according to Crow & Crow, is that via education, students should be able to acquire the appropriate patterns of behaviour for various situations. Man is a social species who must adjust to his surroundings on a regular basis. As a result, education must try to develop all of these attributes in students in order to promote this social adaption. The youngster is self-centred by nature, but education must teach him to consider the wants and requirements of others. One of the characteristics of a well-educated person is the ability to adjust to various conditions in which he feels at ease. The term conduct must be understood in its broadest sense in his situation. Then and only then can this theory of curriculum construction be fully comprehended. "All of our activities in the social, economic, family, and cultural environments combine to form behaviour or conduct, and education's role is to educate us how to behave in various situations."

Principle of synthesis of play and work: -

Some current educational techniques attempt to educate through work, while others attempt to educate through pleasure. However, the vast majority of educators agree that the curriculum should strive for a balance of play and work. To put it another way, the work assigned to the student should be done in such a way that the youngster believes it is play. There is a distinction to be made between work and recreation. As a result, parents prefer to engage their children in work rather than letting them to play all day, but children are naturally motivated to spend their time playing.

Principle of Synthesis of all activities of life: -

When creating a curriculum, it's important to remember to include all of life's activities, such as reflection, learning, and the acquisition of diverse skills. Every individual in the individual and social spheres of life is required to engage in a wide range of activities, and one's success in life is defined by the success of all of these activities. As a result, no activity connected to any part of life should be excluded from the curriculum. A curriculum built on this foundation will be both broad and life-relevant. To put it another way, it should cover all of the activities that a student is likely to need in the future.

Principle of individual differences: -

Individual distinctions that exist between one individual and another have been brought to light and emphasised by modern educational psychology. People differ in their thinking processes, interests, aptitudes, attitudes, abilities, and skills, among other things, and these distinctions are innate. All current education is child-centric, that is, it is focused on the child. According to psychologists, the curriculum should be structured in such a way that it allows for complete and thorough growth for a wide range of people.

Principle of constant development: -

Individual distinctions that exist between one individual and another have been brought to light and emphasised by modern educational psychology. People differ in their thinking processes, interests, aptitudes, attitudes, abilities, and skills, among other things, and these distinctions are innate. All current education is child-centric, that is, it is focused on the child. According to psychologists, the curriculum should be structured in such a way that it allows for complete and thorough growth for a wide range of people.

Principle of creative training: -

Creative training is another significant aspect in curriculum development. Raymont is correct in stating that a curriculum suited for today's and tomorrow's demands must include a strong emphasis on creative disciplines. One of the goals of education is to help students develop their creative abilities. Student. The creation of man's creative powers is the pinnacle of human civilisation. In this regard, children differ from one another. As a result, when designing a curriculum, keep in mind that it should encourage each student to develop his or her creative talent to the fullest extent possible.

Principle of variety: -

Another key concept in curriculum design is variety. Because no single curriculum can develop all of an individual's capabilities, the natural complexity necessitates that the curriculum be valid. As a result, at every level, the curriculum must be varied; on the one hand, it must provide opportunities for the development of the student's many faculties, while on the other, it must maintain his enthusiasm in education.

Principle of education for leisure: -

Another key concept in curriculum design is variety. Because no single curriculum can develop all of an individual's capabilities, the natural complexity necessitates that the curriculum be valid. As a result, at every level, the curriculum must be varied; on the one hand, it must provide opportunities for the development of the student's many faculties, while on the other, it must maintain his enthusiasm in education.

Principle of related to community life: -

Curriculum can also be built around the idea that school and community life must be inextricably linked. It's important to remember that school is merely a miniature version of immunity. As a result, all activities undertaken by members of the greater community outside the school's boundaries should be included in the school curriculum. This will aid in the development of the individual's social qualities, the development of the social part of his own band, and lastly, his final adaptation to the social environment and into which he must ultimately travel.

Principle of evolution of democratic life: -

The necessity to cultivate democratic qualities in individuals drives the development of a curriculum in a democratic society. The curriculum should be so rigorous that it instils a sense of democracy and fosters a positive attitude toward democratic values. The programmes are designed to develop qualities in college students so that they can engage usefully and successfully in democratic society. This is the key factor in developing primary, secondary, and higher education curricula in all democratic countries of the planet.

Objectives of curriculum development

- The curriculum should provide opportunities for a child's whole development. The use of a curriculum can help organise teaching.
- Curriculum must include human experiences, culture, and civilization that will be passed down to future generations.

- Moral character, discipline, honesty, cooperation, friendship, tolerance, and sympathy with others should all be part of the curriculum.
- The curriculum should aid in the development of cognitive talents such as logic, wisdom, and judgement, as well as other mental abilities.
- It should take into account the stages of a child's growth and development in terms of attitude, interest, values, and creative capacity.
- It should promote awareness and comprehension of the physical and social environment, as well as its constituents.
- It should cultivate the appropriate feelings and views about religions, new ideals, and traditions.
- It should assist pupils in developing democratic feelings and a democratic way of life.
- In light of their future lives, it should integrate knowledge from numerous instructional subjects.
- It should establish the manner in which the teacher and students engage in the classroom: The nature of the curriculum determines the manner of instruction.

Steps of curriculum development

Curriculum development is a never-ending or ongoing process. Its outcome is determined by the level of learning achieved by students. It is evaluated on the basis of the learners' changing behaviour.

When it comes to curriculum development, the fundamental goal is to help pupils grow. The programme is meant to help students achieve their goal of changing their behaviour. It is a cyclic process that entails:

- Analysis
- Design
- Selecting
- Formation
- Review

Models of Curriculum Development

Curriculum design can be divided into three types: subject-centered, learner-centered, and problem-centered.

Subject-centered curriculum design focuses on a specific subject or discipline, such as mathematics, literature, or biology. The subject, rather than the student, is the focus of this curriculum design concept. It is the most widely used model of standardised curriculum in K-12 public schools.

Lists of subjects and precise examples of how they should be studied are compiled by teachers. This style is most commonly encountered in big university or college classes when lecturers concentrate on a single subject or discipline.

Lists of subjects and precise examples of how they should be studied are compiled by teachers. This style is most commonly encountered in big university or college classes when lecturers concentrate on a single subject or discipline.

In comparison to other types of curriculum design, subject-centered curriculum design is not student-centered, and the approach is less concerned with individual learning styles. This can lead to issues with student involvement and motivation, as well as a drop-off in pupils who aren't sensitive to this paradigm.

Learner-centered curriculum design, on the other hand, is oriented on the needs, interests, and goals of the students. It recognises that children are not all the same and should not be forced to follow a standardised curriculum in all situations. This strategy tries to give students more control over their education by allowing them to make decisions.

Differentiated instructional plans allow for the selection of timely and relevant assignments, teaching and learning experiences, or activities. Students have been found to be engaged and motivated by this type of curriculum design. The disadvantage of this type of curriculum design is that it can put pressure on teachers to develop content that caters to students' learning requirements and preferences. In a mostly online learning setting, these insights can be difficult to come by. Balancing individual student interests with the course's expected goals may prove difficult.

Students learn how to look at an issue and construct a solution through **problem-centered curriculum design.** A problem-centered curriculum model encourages students to engage in authentic learning by exposing them to real-world situations and abilities that may be applied in the real world. Problem-centered curriculum design has been found to improve curriculum relevance and promote creativity, innovation, and collaboration in the classroom. The disadvantage of this technique is that individual student needs and interests are not always taken into account.

Instructors can choose the model that is best suited to both their students and their course by analysing all three models of curriculum design before they begin planning.

Curriculum development: The Tyler's Model

The Tyler Model is the definitive prototype of curriculum development in the scientific approach, developed by Ralph Tyler in the 1940s. One might virtually argue that every licenced teacher in America, and possibly abroad, has designed curriculum using this paradigm or one of its numerous versions, either directly or indirectly.

Tyler did not aim for his contribution to the curriculum to serve as a development model. Initially, he put his thoughts down in a book called Basic Principles of Curriculum and Instruction for his students to give them an understanding of how to make curriculum. Tyler's model is brilliant since it was one of the first, and it was (and still is) a straightforward four-step process.

- Determine the goals of the school (aka objectives)
- Identify educational experiences that are relevant to your goal.
- Organize the encounters
- Examine the objectives.

Basic principles of curriculum and instruction

The first step is to figure out what the school's or class's goals are. To put it another way, what must students do in order to be successful? Each subject has its own set of natural goals that serve as signs of mastery. All objectives must be congruent with the school's philosophy, which is frequently overlooked in curriculum development. For instance, a school designing an English curriculum would set a goal for pupils to produce essays. This would be just one of the curriculum's numerous goals.

Step two is to create learning experiences that will assist students in completing step one. For instance, suppose students are required to complete an essay. A teacher may demonstrate how to write an essay as part of the learning experience. The kids may then get the opportunity to practise writing essays. The experience (demonstration and writing of an essay) is in line with the goal (Student will write an essay).

The third step is to organise your experiences. Is it better for the teacher to demonstrate initially or for the pupils to learn by writing right away? Either technique could work, and the preference is determined by the teacher's mindset and the students' needs. The point is that the teacher must decide on a logical order for the students' experiences.

The fourth and last phase is to evaluate the objectives. The teacher is now evaluating the students' abilities to compose an essay. This can be accomplished in a variety of ways. For example, the teacher could assign pupils to write an essay on their own. If they are able to do so, it indicates that the students have met the lesson's goal.

Hilda Taba's model of Curriculum Development

'Curriculum,' according to Taba, is a document that contains a statement of the purposes and particular objectives; it indicates certain material selection and structure; and it either implies or exhibits certain learning and teaching patterns. Because the purpose or the content organisation necessitates it, a programme of result evaluation is included.

Strengths of using taba model

- This method makes use of higher-order cognitive abilities.
- Inferencing, synthesising, and summarising skills are all developed.
- Gifted students will benefit from the opportunity to investigate questions that have several correct answers.
- There is no clear right or wrong answer to the question.
- When students are gathered together, they work together to improve their speaking and listening skills.
- Before and after generalisations are made, there is a chance for good classroom debate.

Limitation of using taba model

- The open-ended nature of the concept can be challenging for some students.
- Teachers may find it challenging to plan and prepare questions for the pupils' path if there is no clear direction.
- Adapting to all subjects, or at least some sorts of literature, is difficult.
- Texts must be selected ahead of time.

Conclusion: -

To summarise, curriculum planning for each course is a critical procedure for ensuring correct and consistent knowledge instillation among students. Learners' different needs were taken into account when developing the material and course requirements for EDSE 325 for the spring 2011 curriculum. Because learning would be learner-centered to a large extent, this was designed to boost morale and interest in learning.

Though the curriculum was developed in a frantic manner, much was realised and accomplished. Because my profession is teaching, the skills and knowledge I've received will be extremely useful in my future attempts. It is crucial to remember that the curriculum should take into account the classroom's productivity and safety in order to ensure that all of the learners' demands are met efficiently.

References: -

- www.vkmaheshwari.com/WP/?p=1833/
- https://www.skyepack.com/post/curriculum-development/
- https://tophat.com/blog/curriculum-development-models-design/
- https://educationalresearchtechniques.com/2014/07/01/curriculum/
- https://www.educarepk.com/taba-model-of-curriculum-development.html/
- https://ivypanda.com/essays/curriculum-development-essay/

CHAPTER XIX

Phases and Steps in Curriculum Development

****Dr.Mukta Goyal**

• • •

Introduction

As any instructor knows, the writing and reasoning encompassing the idea of an educational plan have developed throughout the long term. Today the term can be extensively used to incorporate the whole arrangement for a course, including the learning targets, showing systems, materials, and evaluations.

By and large, educational program improvement is the interaction by which an educator or foundation makes or takes on that arrangement for a course. Since this subject is so wide, it very well may be challenging to swim through the clamor to find cutting-edge prescribed procedures. There are likewise many ways of thinking for how best to move toward the educational plan advancement process.

Educational program improvement is the multi-step interaction of making and further developing a course instructed at an everyday schedule. While the specific cycle will fluctuate from one foundation to another, the expansive structure incorporates phases of examination, building, execution, and assessment.

In K-12 schools, educational plans are frequently evolved at a neighborhood or state level to bring about normalized learning results across various schools. At the school level, teachers might get more individual adaptability to foster their own educational plans. Regardless, the individual or gathering is liable for arranging a course (and picking solid relating course materials) that actually achieves instructive objectives and addresses understudy issues.

Preferably, the educational plan advancement interaction ought to be one of persistent improvement as opposed to a straight or stale methodology. Plans for guidance ought to be every now and again checked on, changed, and refreshed as required. Change might be expected because of branch of knowledge disclosures, advancements in informative accepted procedures, or changes in direction conveyance like the turn to remote educating

Educational program advancement is a wide and complex interaction. In any case, what is educational program precisely? A few are the responses given to this inquiry. For example, Bobbit (1918) in Angulo (1994) characterized educational program in two ways. The first is as

the scope of encounters coordinated to foster abilities in the people. The other one is as the series of preparing encounters that schools use to finish and wonderful that turn of events. Following this line, Tyler (1949) in Portuondo (1997) guaranteed that educational program is all the opportunities for growth arranged and guided by the school to come to the school's instructive objectives. Additionally, Arrieta (1995) in Angulo (1994) characterized educational program as the series of things that youngsters and teens need to perform and experience to foster capacities that would frame them to choose issues in their life as grown-ups. Being more unambiguous, Taba (1974) in Montoya (1997) expressed that generally, educational program is a learning plan. This learning plan, as per Taba (1962) in Portuondo (1997) is made by a few components which incorporate the foundation of objectives and goals, etermination and association of content, ramifications of learning and showing designs, and an outcomes assessment program.

Why is a concrete curriculum development strategy valuable for learners?

In expansion to giving advantages to instructors, educational plan improvement is a valuable design for students.

Educational program improvement permits educators to adopt a smart and deliberate strategy to figure out what understudies will be expected to learn. The beginning stages of the cycle include profound exploration and examination to guarantee that understudies get the most ideal training.

Furthermore, one of the best methodologies for course improvement explicitly addresses the necessities of students. We'll cover the student-focused plan later in this article.

Are there various educational program improvement cycles or models?

To start with, there are for the most part two kinds of educational plan models: the item model and the cycle model. The model you decide to follow will impact the means you'll take to foster the course.

Whole reading material have been composed on these well-established models, yet here's a concise clarification of each to ensure everybody is in total agreement:

Product model. Otherwise called the goals model, this model spotlights on assessments, results, and results. It figures out what realizing has happened. Assuming you really want to foster an educational plan that focuses on government sanctioned test scores, you'll have to stick to the item model. For the most part, this model is believed to be more unbending and more challenging to adjust to your understudies' extraordinary requirements, however it gives quantitative learning evaluations.

Process model. This model spotlights on how learning creates over the long run. There's an accentuation on how the understudies are learning, and what contemplations they have all through the interaction. This approach is more open-finished and considers the general development and improvement of an understudy as opposed to their presentation on a test.

Consider the qualities of each model as the need might arise to stick to. You may as of now have a solid inclination for one of the two! Fostering an educational program that values both item and process is additionally conceivable.

Whenever you've figured out what sort of educational plan you need to make, now is the ideal time to pick a methodology. There are three broadly acknowledged systems for educational plan:

1. Subject-focused
2. Issue focused
3. Student-focused

We'll investigate every one of these more meticulously later on with the goal that you can figure out which educational plan improvement procedure checks out for your course.

Phases and Steps in Curriculum

(See Figure 1) for a visual representation of how the 12 essential steps progress from one to the next. It also depicts the interaction and relationships between the four key stages of the curriculum development process:

I. Planning,
II. Content and Methods, and
III. Evaluation
IV. implementation, as well as

V. Assessment and Reporting It is critical to recognize that things do not always work exactly as they are depicted in a model!

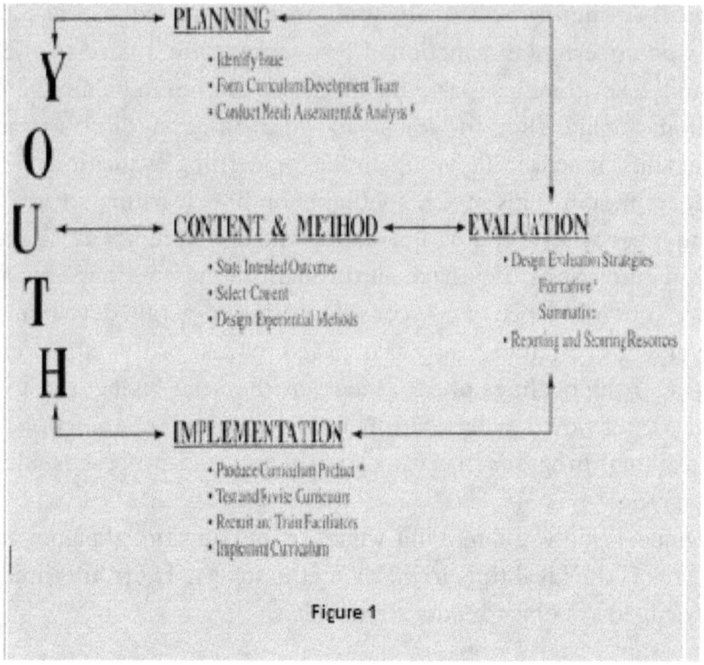

fao.org

Each phase has several steps or tasks that must be done in a logical order. These steps are not always separate and distinct, but they can overlap and occur simultaneously. For example, the curriculum development team participates in all steps. Most of the steps involved in evaluating progress should include evaluations. The team learns what works and what doesn't and determines the impact of the curriculum on students once it is implemented. Each step logically follows the previous one. It would not make sense to design learning activities before student outcomes and content have been described and identified. Also, the content cannot be determined until the learning outcomes are described.

Based on the author's experience and confirmed by other curriculum specialists, the next steps in curriculum development are often overlooked or neglected. These steps are essential to the successful development of the curriculum and should be emphasized.

Essential Curriculum Development Steps to Highlight

1. Needs Assessment

: If not done, a wonderful curriculum could be developed, but the appropriate needs of the target audience may not be met.

2. Youth Involvement: The target audience and volunteers (or staff) implementing the curriculum must participate (ie participate as full members of the curriculum development team).

3. Recruitment and training of volunteer facilitators: Competent and experienced curriculum implementers are crucial (the printed word cannot teach an experiential group process, there is no feedback).

4. Curriculum Impact Assessment and Reporting - Critical to ensure human and financial support from key policy makers and to assess whether the curriculum has achieved its intended results.

Two types of assessment are included in the description of the phases and steps:

(1) Formative gives feedback during the curriculum development process and

(2) Summative answers questions about changes (effects) that students experience as a result of their learning experiences. Summative evaluation provides evidence of what works, what doesn't, and what needs improvement.

At every step of the curriculum development process, the most important task is to monitor the students (in this case, the youth) and involve them in the process. For example, members of the curriculum team who are directly familiar with the target group should be involved in conducting the needs assessment. From the needs analysis process, problem areas are identified, gaps between what young people know and what they need to know are identified, and the scope of the problem is clarified and defined. The results can lead decision makers to allocate resources to a curriculum development team to prepare curriculum materials.

The following is a brief description of each step in the development of the curriculum. After reviewing these descriptions, you should have a clear idea of how each step works and what each step entails.

Phase 1:Planning

"No one plans to fail, but failure is the result of a failure in planning."

The planning phase forms the foundation of all steps in the development of the curriculum. Steps in this phase include:

(1) Identify problem / problem / need

The need for curriculum development generally arises out of concern for an important issue or problem from one or more target groups. This section examines some of the questions that must be addressed to define the problem and develop an explanation that will guide the selection of members of a curriculum development team. The topic is also used to roughly determine the scope (what will be included) of the content of the curriculum.

(2) Curriculum development team form

Once the type and scope of the topic have been roughly defined, members of the curriculum development team can be selected. Topics covered in this section include:

- the roles and functions of team members,
- a process for selecting members of the curriculum development team, and
- principles of collaboration and teamwork. The goal is to gain the expertise of team members in the areas included in the curriculum and to develop a powerful team.

(3) Conduct Needs Assessment and Analysis

The Needs Assessment process consists of two phases. The first are the procedures for conducting a needs assessment. Various techniques are intended to learn what is needed and who needs it in relation to the identified problem. Techniques covered in this section include: CAP Knowledge, Attitudes, and Practices Survey; Focus groups; and environmental scanning.

Analysis, the second part of this needs assessment step, describes techniques for using the data and results of the collected information. These include: ways to identify gaps between knowledge and practice; Trends emerging from the data; a process to prioritize needs; and identify the characteristics of the target audience.

"As the branch bends, the tree grows"

Phase II : Content And Methods

Phase II determines the desired outcomes (what students can do after participating in the curriculum activities), content (what is taught), and methods (how it is taught). Steps include:

(4) State Expected Results Once the topic is defined, the curriculum team is established, needs are assessed, analyzed, and prioritized, the next step is to refine and rephrase the topic based on as necessary and develop the expected results or educational goals. An expected result indicates what the student can do as a result of her participation in the curriculum activities.

This section contains:

- A definition of expected outcomes,
- Components of expected outcomes (condition, performance, and standards),
- Examples of expected outcomes, and
- An overview of learning behavior . A more detailed explanation of the types and levels of learning behavior is included in the appendix, as well as examples of expected results from the FAO population training materials.

(5) Content Selection

The next challenge in the curriculum development process is choosing content that truly changes the lives of students and, ultimately, society as a whole. At this point, the most important questions are: "What does the student need to know to achieve the desired result? What knowledge, skills, attitudes and behaviors do they need to acquire and practice?"

The scope (breadth of knowledge, skills, attitudes and behaviors) and the order (sequence) of the contents are also discussed. The desired population training outcomes with content topics are provided in the Addendum section as an example and an application of how the expected results are linked to the content.

(6) Experimenting with the method design

After selecting the content, the next step is to design activities (learning experiences) to help the student achieve the appropriate intended results. This section covers an experiential learning model and its components (that is, experiment, share, process, generalize, and apply).

Additional topics include:

- Learning styles and activities that are appropriate for each style;
- A list of types of activities (with descriptions);
- A worksheet for designing activities for facilitators; and

- Short discussions on learning environments and modes of delivery.

The appendix includes ten sample population training worksheets and tips for facilitators who work with young people on sensitive topics.

Phase III: Implementation

(7) Create Curriculum Product

Once the content and experience-based methods have been agreed upon, actual production of curriculum materials begins. This section contains: 1) tips for finding and evaluating existing materials; 2) evaluation criteria; and 3) suggestions for the creation of curricular materials.

(8) Curriculum Review and Review

This step provides suggestions for selecting exam locations and conducting a formative assessment of curriculum materials during the production phase. A sample evaluation form will be provided.

(9) Recruitment and training of facilitators

It is a waste of resources to develop curriculum materials if facilitators are not properly trained to implement them. Suggestions for hiring suitable facilitators are provided with an exemplary three-day training program.

(10) Curriculum Implementation

Effective implementation of newly developed curriculum products is unlikely without planning. In this step, strategies for promoting and using the curriculum are discussed.

Phase IV: Evaluation And Reports

(11) Design of evaluation strategies

Evaluation is a phase of the curriculum development model and a specific step. Two types of assessments are used during curriculum development, formative and summative. Formative assessments are used during needs analysis, product development, and testing steps. Summative assessments are conducted to measure and report on the results of the curriculum. In this step, the evaluation strategies are reviewed and simple procedures are proposed to obtain valid and reliable information. A series of questions are formulated to guide the summative evaluation process and a sample evaluation format is suggested.

(12) Reporting and obtaining resources

The final element of an evaluation strategy is "getting the payoff (that is, putting the results in the hands of people who can use them). This step makes suggestions on what and how "a briefing for key stakeholders, particularly policy and financing decision makers, and a brief discussion on securing resources for additional programs

Conclusion

Educational plan advancement is definitely not a straightforward and consistent cycle. All things considered, it is a perplexing, changing, and continuous interaction that requires bunches of examination from educational program engineers. Accordingly, educational program designers need to think about quite a large number viewpoints while creating educational program. They should investigate the social powers like legislative issues, economy, culture, history, innovation, and religion as well as the instructive powers. The instructive powers incorporate logicians and their philosophical flows, the educational plan designer's way of thinking as well as the understudies, society, and the actual subject that sway the educational plan in the time it is being created. Likewise, they should have a wide comprehension about the requirements of the educational plan. These necessities include the general public, understudies, and the subject's requirements at a particular time as life and time advance. Besides, it is likewise important that they know who the people that impact the improvement of any educational program are as well as the degree of force they have. At long last, information going to plan, execute, and assess the educational program and the steps that are important for that educational plan improvement interaction or cycle ought to be perceived by the educational program engineers. Also, educational program improvement can be created at various levels beginning from the homeroom to school, locale, zone, and country levels. Educators themselves are educational program engineers when they plan their classes, they are

Creating educational program. To summarize, educational program advancement is definitely not a secluded cycle. It is created at various levels and requires an incredible arrangement of information in regards to the assortment of angles that mediate in its interaction. Besides, educational program can't be created by one single individual. It is a helpful gathering work. Subsequently, to foster an educational plan it is vital the particiaption of many individuals beginning from the understudies, the local area, subject trained professionals, school staff, what's more, society overall as hotspots for educational plan improvement.

References

- Schneiderhan, J., Guetterman, T. C., & Dobson, M. L. (2019). Curriculum development: a how to primer. *Family Medicine and Community Health,*

7(2).

- Correa, R. (2012, July 19). Firma convenio examenes TOFEL-IBT. [Lecture]. Presidencia de la republica del Ecuador. Retrieved August 30, 2014, from http://www.presidencia.gob.ec/wp-content/uploads/downloads/2012/10/2012-07-19-Firmade-Co
- https://files.eric.ed.gov/fulltext/EJ1095725.pdf
- Soto, S. T. (2015). An analysis of curriculum development. *Theory and Practice in Language Studies, 5*(6), 1129.
- Richards, J. C. (1984). Language curriculum development. *RELC journal, 15*(1), 1-29.
- Kern, D. E., Thomas, P. A., Bass, E. B., & Howard, D. M. (1998). *Curriculum development for medical education: a six step approach.* JHU Press.
- Modebelu, M. N. (2015). Curriculum Development Models for Quality Educational System. In *Handbook of research on enhancing teacher education with advanced instructional technologies* (pp. 259-276). IGI Global.
- https://www.skyepack.com/post/curriculum-development]
- Convenio de Cooperacion Interinstitucional entre la Secretaria Nacional de Educacion Superior, Ciencia, Tecnologia e Innovacion y el Ministerio de Educacion-20120281. (2012). Quito, Ecuador: SENESCYT & Ministerio de Educación Ecuador.
- Gomez, C., & Salvador, C. C. (1994). De que hablamos cuando hablamos de constructivismo. Cuadernos de Pedagogia, 221, 8-10.
- Haboud, M. (2009). Teaching foreign languages: A challenge to Ecuadorian bilingual intercultural education. International Journal of English Studies, 9, 63-80.

CHAPTER XX

Curriculum Development Models

Mr.Anand Prakash Dube,*Swati Singh

• • •

Introduction

An educational plan is an unpredictable wonder it needs to foster a comprehension of the hypothetical viewpoint and make it important and have its utilitarian worth to the understudies. Educational program is a Design, Plan of discovery that requires the intentional and Proactive association, Sequencing and Management of the collaborations among the Teacher, student, and the substance Knowledge we need Students to gain. A model is a configuration for Curriculum configuration created to address special issues settings or purposes. To accomplish these objectives, Curriculum engineers plan, reconfigure or rework at least one key educational program parts.

Objectives:

After going through this substance, Students will actually want to: -

1. Comprehend the educational plan models

2. Separate between the specialized and non-specialized models of educational plan improvement

3. Depict the MODEL OF CURRICULUM DEVELOPMENT

MODEL OF CURRICULUM DEVELOPMENT:

Curriculum model is an expansive term alluding to the reports utilized in training to decide the particular parts of educating, like subject, time period, and 2 way of guidance. A Curriculum model decides the kind of educational program utilized it envelops instructive way of thinking, way to deal with instructing, and technique. The accomplishment of our instructive undertakings lays on cautious arranging, without which issue and turmoil will result. The need to design viable educational programs can't be denied. From such educational program producers designs a model for educational plan improvement. For the development of an educational plan, thought ought to be given to objectives, content, learning encounters, procedure and assessment. Curricular methodologies likewise center around various perspectives like topic and society. Models can be named either specialized or logical models and non-specialized or non-logical models

Technical or scientific models –

Instructors who stress subject, matter methodologies embrace the logical or specialized methodology for the educational plan improvement. Educational plan engineers planned this methodology by utilizing the logical model which requires noticing and checking of parts. These parts are topics, destinations, learning encounters and assessment. In this methodology, educational program advancement is a helpful BluePrint for organizing the learning climate. Specialized or logical models as follows:

1. Hilda Taba Model
2. Tyler Model
3. Saylor Alexander Model
4. Goodlad Model
5. Hunkins Model
6. Mill operator and Seller Model

Non-specialized or non-logical –

Educators who accentuate students and issues detail non-specialized or non-logical educational plan plans. It has been depicted as Subjective, Personal, Esthetic and spotlights on student needs and topic and society, become optional.

Three models under this classification:

1. Open Classroom Model
2. Wienstien and Fantini Model
3. Roger's Model of Interpersonal Relations

TABA - MODEL OF CURRICULUM DEVELOPMENT

The Taba Model was created by Hilda Taba (1902 – 1967), an engineer, an educational plan scholar, an educational program reformer, and an instructor teacher. She was brought into the world in the little town of Kooraste, Estonia. Taba accepted that there must be a distinct request in making an educational plan.

Hilda Taba is the engineer of the Taba Model of learning. This model is utilized to improve the considering abilities understudies. Hilda Taba accepted that there should be a cycle for evalutating understudy accomplishment of content after the substance norms have been set up and executed. The fundamental idea of this way to deal with educational plan advancement is that educators should be engaged with the improvement of the educational program.

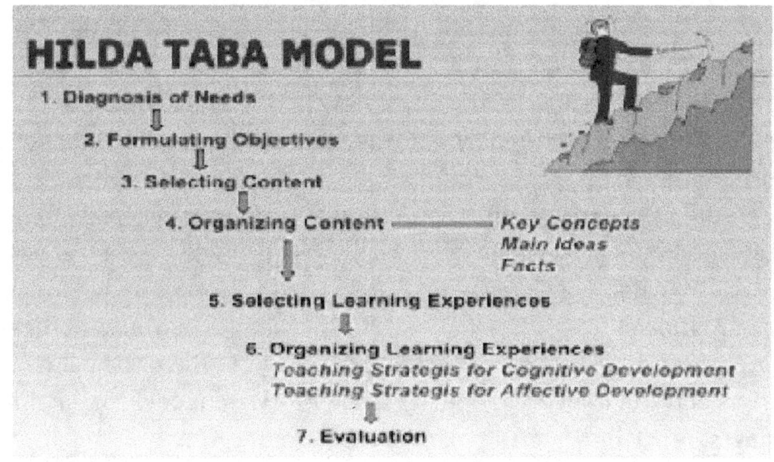

Educare

Strengths of using the Taba Model in the classroom:

- Skilled understudies start thinking about an idea, then, at that point jump further into that idea
- Spotlights on open-finished inquiries as opposed to right/wrong inquiries
- The open-endedness requires more theoretical reasoning, an advantage to our skilled understudies
- The inquiries and answers loan themselves to rich homeroom conversation
- Simple to evaluate understudy learning

Limitations of using the Taba Model in the classroom:

- Can be hard for non-skilled understudies to get a handle on
- Hard for heterogeneous homerooms
- Functions admirably for fiction and genuine, might be hard to handily use in all subjects

Curriculum Development: The Tyler Model

The Tyler Model, created by Ralph Tyler in the 1940's, is the quintessential model of educational plan advancement in the logical methodology. One could nearly set out to say that each guaranteed instructor in America and perhaps past has created educational plan either straightforwardly or in a roundabout way utilizing this model or one of the numerous varieties.

Tyler didn't mean for his commitment to educational plan to be a lockstep model for advancement. Initially, he recorded his thoughts in a book Basic Principles of Curriculum and Instruction for his understudies to give them a thought regarding standards for to making educational program. The brightness of Tyler's model is that it was one of the principal models and it was and still is an exceptionally straightforward model comprising of four stages.

- Decide the school's motivations (otherwise known as goals).
- Recognize instructive encounters identified with reason
- Sort out the encounters
- Assess the reasons

What is Tyler Model of Curriculum

Tyler Model of Curriculum was created by the American teacher Ralph Tyler during the 1940s. He presented this strategy for educational program advancement in his book Basic Principles of Curriculum and Instruction. It was one of the primary models of educational plans and a straightforward model even utilized by current instructors.

Tyler model of educational program portrays how to detail instructive destinations, how to arrange them, break down them and change them so the understudies can meet these goals. Fundamentally, Tyler introduced his educational program reasoning as four inquiries:

- What instructive purposes should the school try to accomplish?
- What instructive encounters can be given that will probably achieve these reasons?
- How could these instructive encounters be viably coordinated?
- How might we decide if the reasons for existing are being accomplished?

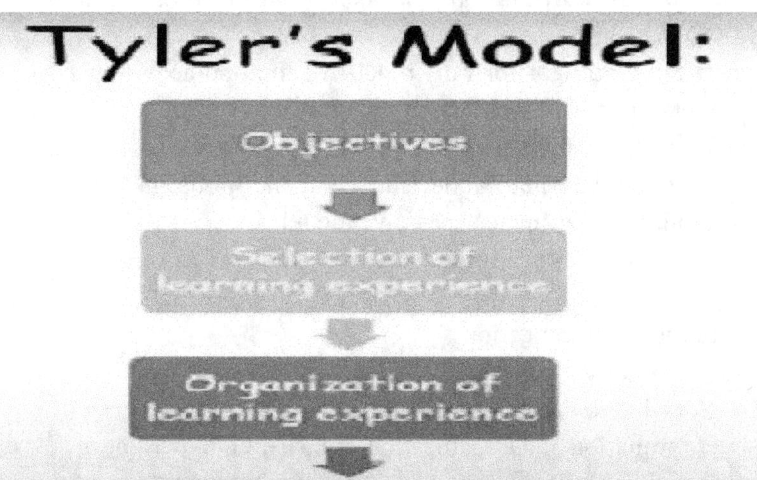

foolaa

As indicated by Tylor, in fostering any educational plan ought to include responding to these four inquiries. In addition, this model is direct in nature, and targets structure the essential segment in the educational plan improvement. Additionally, goals are the reason for the determination and association of learning encounters, and they structure the reason for surveying the educational plan. Besides, destinations are gotten from the student, contemporary life and subject trained professional. Consequently, we likewise call this model the goal model.

We can likewise re-form these four inquiries into four standards as follows:

- Characterizing proper learning target
- Building up helpful learning encounters
- Sorting out learning encounters to have a greatest total impact
- Assessing the educational program and changing the viewpoints that didn't end up being powerful

Nicholls And Nicholls - 1972 Model

Audrey and Howard Nicholls, his book "Fostering a Curriculum Practical Guide"(1978)

concocted a straight forward repetitive methodology that covered the components of educational plan momentarily however, briefly. This model resembles a guide for specific instructing and learning measure. It is a repeating model (normal Model and Dynamic model in center of it this model stand. It is legitimate successive model

Components of educational plan are associated in this model

Steps:

1. Situational investigation
2. Determinations of Objectives
3. Determination and Organization of Content
4. Determination and Organization of Learning Experiences
5. Assessment

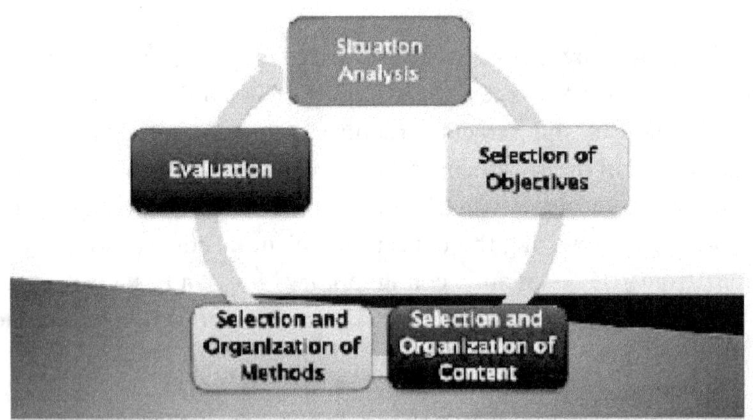

Slideshare

Situational Analysis.

This progression incorporate information about the climate where the educational program will be executed, the social construction of that society, the customs and requirements of the local area.

Selection of Objectives.

1. Goals ought to be sensible.

2. Extent of objective ought to be wide.

3. Destinations ought to be clear and valuable.

4. Objective ought to foster both sort of conduct for example expected and content

5. Objective should empower understudies to perform abilities

Determination and Organization of Content.

At the point when targets are chosen it is not difficult to go for the determination of content.

1. Content should be in arrangement.

2. Content should be substantial and solid

3. Content should satisfy the requirements of society

4. Content should be not difficult to troublesome

5. Content should be as per the psychological degree of understudies

6. Content should be age same

At the point when the substance is chosen it should be coordinated

1. Successive request

2. Easy to complex

3. Simple to troublesome

4. Known to obscure

5. Prompt to far off

Choice and Organization of Learning Experiences

1. It gives understudies freedom to self-action so that move information acquired furthermore, expertise procured.

2. It gives understudies chance of free reasoning and dynamic.

3. It ought to be adjusted by the necessities of understudies so they acquire fulfillment.

4. It ought to be orchestrated in habits that give progression and connection.

5. It ought to be viable, intriguing and valuable for the understudies.

At the point when the learning encounters are chosen it ought to be coordinated

1. Presentation, opener, direction

2. Improvement, investigation, study

3. Speculation

4. Application, rundown

5. Mood of learning exercises

Assessment

Various strategies and approaches of assessment are utilized to check the advancement of understudies.

1. Test
2. Quiz
3. Show
4. Viva

Benefits

1. In the present circumstance as it implies that teachers can
2. Consistently return to their work and make changes, rather
3. Then, at that point return to the start and start again every time there
4. It Is even the littlest of changes expected to the educational plan.
5. Sensible consecutive association
6. Situational Analysis is in initial step
7. It is a Flexible model

Weaknesses

1. Tedious, as situational examination is long time measure
2. Hard to keep up with sensible successive examination

References:

- https://www.studocu.com/row/document/bahauddin-zakariya-university/curriculum-development/lecture-notes/cyclical-models-of-curriculum-development/10087807/view
- http://kausapatel.blogspot.com/2016/03/nicholls-and-nicholls-1972-model.html
- https://www.scribd.com/document/443158649/Nicholls-and-Nicholls
- https://pediaa.com/what-is-the-difference-between-tyler-and-wheeler-model-of-curriculum/
- http://www.vkmaheshwari.com/WP/?p=1894
- https://educationalresearchtechniques.com/2014/07/01/curriculum-development-the-tyler-model/
- https://norhazwanishuib.wordpress.com/2017/06/18/reflective-3-taba-model-of-curriculum-development-efland-theory-cognitive/
- http://www.meerutcollege.org/mcm_admin/upload/1587313785.pdf
- https://www.patnauniversity.ac.in/e-content/education/Med53.pdf

CHAPTER XXI

A Practical Approach To Curriculum Development: A Case Study

Mr. K. C. Malik,* Kanishka Tomar

Introduction

Changes in society continuously call for the growth of our education system and for new knowledge and skills. How do study development procedures evolve? In actuality, what is a curriculum? And how can the quality of curricular goods be guaranteed? These questions will be addressed in this book. The first attempt to condense our curriculum development expertise for our SLO colleagues can also give a clear and short introduction into the techniques of curriculum development business to teachers, educators, policymakers and other stakeholders interested in educational development. The book addresses fundamental principles in the construction of curricula and gives valuable frames of thought and strategy. The development of curriculum means a local, regional or state/ provincial process, which is sometimes difficult for teachers to understand (Hansen, Fliesser, Froelich, & McClain, 1992).

image.shutterstock.com

In their view, the authorities (e.g., regional advisory board members or school writing teams) have years of education system expertise. The teacher's expectations are often that the knowledge, talents and attitudes of a particular topic or vocation be taught and transferred effectively. Educators who have been in the trade for years know differently. Successful teaching practice has an inextricable connection with the construction of curricula - daily decisions regarding both teaching and teaching.

It is deliberate to use technological education as the analytical unit of this study. In the middle of an unparalleled curriculum change in schools, technological education is underway. Pragmatically, the origins of the reform are many. Firstly, technology altered itself (Bell, 1989). Bell identifies four innovations underlying what it describes as a Third Technology Revolution: the transition from electronic, electronic and mechanical systems to electronic systems; miniaturization-invention and use of semiconductors for machinery and process monitoring and regulation; digitization-conversion from digital to analogue systems to improvement in system performance; Secondly, in schools, education technology is changing. New technologies have provided teachers and students an opportunity to find new ways of learning, particularly through utilizing their computer as a teacher. Thirdly, new concepts for teacher development change (Feiman-Nemser, 1990). Teacher training is more closely linked to the design of curriculum at the levels of school, in particular technical education, as is previously carried out in any school subject or programme area.

A process evaluation is intended to offer a guarantee of quality of the product.

Assessing the process of curriculum building plays an essential role in leading and keeping the young generation on the correct track to achieve the national objectives and keeping the system up to date with changing time circumstances. New progress has also altered the curricular design process and retains its validity, confidence and direction as a consequence of its evaluation. Evaluation recommendations for all processes have an eternal message. The requirement is thus to structure the process to prepare young women and men for higher education and to enable them to make a meaningful and productive adjustment to their practical life. Because the educational aims can only be achieved via a credible curriculum and a competent evaluation of the process for the updating and fulfilment of essential society needs.

Due to the misunderstanding between the objectives, starting points, methodologies and functions of external and user development, deficiencies of "top down" techniques in curricular development and local user-based curriculum development arise. The objective of outside development is the construction and transposition into coherent curricular resources of theoretical conceptions of society, knowledge, instructors, teachers and learners. The role of user development is to create pictures of certain instructional settings in accordance with a number of theory concepts and to transform them into a curricular usage. Harmonious performance would provide a measure of progressive development in the practice of educational curricula.

The word "curriculum" is used in several ways. The Dictionary of Concise Oxford describes it as a study path and says that it originates from the Latin language of a chariot race. Many of you still have a perspective today of your curriculum as a race with a variety of "hurdles" to overcome. Printing, printing (1993, p.110) For the professional teacher, the curriculum is an area of critical importance. The curriculum study has been an integral element of teacher training in the last two decades. Teachers therefore need to be aware of the curricula and to comprehend how the curricula may be drawn up. For example, teachers address the essential topic of education which may be discussed with regard to core curricular concerns.

(I)What do I want to teach?

(ii) How can I be taught?

(iii) When is it necessary to teach?

(iv) How does teaching influence?

Which knowledge is the most important? What are the most successful teaching activities to collect this knowledge (information, facts, skills, values, attitudes, etc.)? The best method to arrange these events is by wheat. How can I know whether this information has been acquired?

Good features of the curriculum:

The good curriculum has the following properties:

• Social understanding development

• Enhancement of maximum personal development

• Encouragement of continuity of education

• Maintenance of the balance of goals

• Use of the efficient experience of learning and resources required

Curriculum Evaluation refers to the collecting of information on which the value and efficiency of a certain curriculum may be assessed. Of course, it also entails making such judgements, in order to decide if the software is to be retained, changed or discarded as it stands. In his analysis, he finds the four key elements for evaluation provided under: Stocked deals with the curriculum assessment through a conceptual review of the term "evaluation".

1. Evaluation is an assessment that we assess.

2. In light of the criteria, such decisions are made.

3. Criteria are the subject of specific material and are suitable.

4. Such criteria encompass human resources and hence guide judgments on the assessment model.

Important approaches and methods used to assess the curriculum include discussions, experiments, interviews (groups and stakeholders), observation processes, surveys, practice and formal records of many organizations involved.

The significance of goals in the creation of curricula

lh3.googleusercontent.com/

This article shows that an improvement in the efficiency of the curriculum should be based on a curricular framework that is based on a number of specific objectives. While there are few standards to describe how to build curricula that focus on the improved abilities, past research on enhanced skills and assessment at certain institutions defines new curricula. We think major curriculum changes can be made in this way. The article provides an example of a curriculum structure containing a corporate core, an accounting core, and an accounting degree. Our technique proposed includes the setting of educational programme goals, followed by the definition of evaluable programme objective subsets. One consequence of this curriculum structure is that the evaluation should be conducted largely at the level of the course.

The study's major goals were as follows:

a) The evaluation of the curriculum creation process must produce an effective sketch of the elements involved.

b) Supporting the establishment of a continuous curricular process assessment system.

(c) point out the institutions accountable that can successfully carry out future curriculum development work.

d) Estimating the performance of institutions participating in the creation of curricula.

e) To evaluate the current process of curriculum development

Importance of the trial

Curricula are a continuous process and required modifications are part of the process to make changing requirements more responsive and relevant. There is no question that the successful process of curriculum creation may increase participant learning. Evaluations may only be made if they are properly initiated with regard to the drafting, execution. When the planned evaluation is essential to evaluate, perceive and improve planning and execution of existing and future activities, it will help the majority of research projects undertaken on curricula.

Development of curricula

The construction of the curriculum may be an amazing effort that involves many hours of teaching and enormous stacks of documents. But if they are to be up to date in business and educational trends, all hospitality programmes must do so. This article describes a method for curriculum reform step-by-step. This will be particularly beneficial for professors and managers who wish to lead the process and it offers a practical way to manage the curriculum vitae.

Curative Development Principles

The ideas by which the study has evolved stem from the early decades of this century. In Bobbitt's opinion (1918) education might be reduced to an efficient method, since the process of industry and mass media creation were at that time commonly understood by educators. Only Tyler (1949) established a disciplined method to teaching did the paradigm of curriculum making alter, which had dominated for half a century. In the 1950s and 1960s, education psychologists, among others, acquired significant respect, as behavioral goals led to a set of principles to guide the education process. The currency of choice in texts regarding modern education was narrow concerns with specific and abstract curricular aspects (e.g., targets, teaching and measuring techniques). Goodlad (1958) argued for a complete and consistent curriculum design framework, the only exception to what would certainly be called curriculum theory. In 1972, Schwab endorsed Goodlad's demand for a conceptual structure for decision-making in the curriculum. He accused theory of generating a disappointing condition of study and practical studies. Progress, he said, will begin from a thorough knowledge of existing behaviors and their impacts rather than a monolithic change. By the late 1970s it was fair to claim that curriculum design was on the brink of developing as an area of study if not curriculum theory.

In the literature on education there is a great deal of discussion on the significance and role of curricular theory and curriculum development

(Barrow 1984; Goodlad 1984; Pratt 1994; Miller & Seller 1985). Barrow offered a good view on the discussion:

The concept of curriculum design is otiose: in the sense of persons competent at officially stating how curricula should be established, or defining an invariance of stages in the formulation of the curriculum, we do not want curricular designers. We want individuals to smartly develop specific courses. Many of the distinctions between designers and design concepts are mostly unimportant, as they raise concerns as to how to best deal with the problem and how to have the best influence, rather than how to create a unified curriculum plan.

The author believes that curricula is necessarily an intricate idea that is addressed with equal challenge and enthusiasm, theory and practice, as is somewhat represented in the following curricular principles. Teacher educational programmes might need to reconsider the significance and location of curricular theory in order to appropriately handle that complexity. As Apple (1990) and Goodson (1991) point out, there are well-understood concepts of how curriculum theory is lead educational transformation. Often it appears quite rational and sensitive to justify the overall direction of a curriculum strategy in schools or the actual result differs from what has been planned. Whether one takes Goodson's (1991) concept that theory of curriculum, to use it, must begin with school and teaching or Apple's (1990) view that we are restricted to the political and cultural forces that are profoundly integrated in the schools, the ultimate effect is the same.

Since resume and curriculum change are complicated, teacher development researchers in the University of Western Ontario regarded both curricular and curricular development to be physical processes at the teacher and educational levels requiring an eclectic and applied approach. Until recently, the ideology of the curriculum in technology education was neglected in the aforementioned context (Layton, 1993). Zuga's work (1993) and Herschbach's work (1992) is very beneficial to draw out the theory of technological education and the field of design. Herschbach states that "conceptual inconsistency has been a feature of the movement [variations in technology education, technical/utilitarian or skills-based curricular design]". He believes that the curriculum-design pattern, which should underlie technological training, should underpin discussion (academic rationalism, technical/utilitarian, intellectual, social reconstruction, or personal significance). The capacity to handle tools, use materials and implement mechanical processes, should be more widely defined in Herschbach's opinion than "competences. Problem solving, talents for critical thinking, organized working methods are skills that can also be recognized" (p. 26). Against the wish of Mr. Herschbach to establish a "process design pattern" for technology education, Mr. Zuga (1993) proposes a range of ideas. While acknowledging the necessity to amend Kliebard (1992) categories to include the rise of poste-modern philosophy (social efficiency, human development, social meliorism), Zuga points out that technology training programmes are mostly an example of the social paradigm of efficiency:

I believe that our theory has to be diversified. The positive idea of one truth, one path, one philosophy, one united profession is a problem. The idea of social efficiency is based on positive theoretical principles, but never serves a varied population's different demands; instead, positivist theory tries to make everything uniform.... I see no reason why a single philosophy of technology education should be based on a single course.

The basis for the establishment of curricular guidelines

Practices are essential in such a situation. First, a conceptual environment to organize learning activities and develop curricula might be more important than is now recognized in a professor's preparation (Feiman-Nemser, 1990). The student literature did not pay the attention it needs to the curriculum (Haughey, 1992; Pratt, 1994; Sanders, 1990). Second, prospective technology instructors should be able to think about their own ideas and attitudes towards learning (Hansen, 1995). According to Feiman-Nemser, the insight obtained via a means of conceptualizing personal attitudes and beliefs in learning is a vital part of teacher development. This is particularly the case in technological education due to the diverse character of the belief systems maintained by professionals with business and industrial backgrounds and ideological trends. Third, an epistemological basis for technology education has to be explored. However, the gap between knowledge and practice is crucial for educators in the construction of an epistemological and educational justification for technologic education (Savage & Sterry, 1990). Fourthly, it is important to understand, fully grasp and consistently use the curriculum creation process at all levels of schools. For years, the approach of problem analysis for creating curricula (Fryklund, 1970) was an important element of technical teacher training. While work analysis was outdated, additional efforts are needed to discover and establish its value in today's technology-centered culture for the genealogy of scientific curriculum (Kliebard, 1992). Lauda (1994) alludes to the necessity for a global knowledge which is appropriately central to the technology study while not using the term technocentric. Finally, the idea that prospective teachers need to grasp the political reality linked to curricular work is probably more prominent. Education policy is a topic of study ignored in the curriculum for teacher education. It is less understood and addressed, yet important for successful curriculum implementation.

The structure of this article coincides with the following five locations. Each assumption is investigated and a principle is established to improve the practice in creation of curricula. Although each concept is presented by the reader as a separate entity for focus and clarity (much like a literary sketch). The guiding principles articulated above (that is, the need to provide a framework for conceptual research, opportunities to reflect attitudes and beliefs, an exploration of the theme's epistemological basis, the process of curricula development and the understanding of the political realities).

Principle 1: Essence of design of curricula The Conceptual Framework Need

Like education in its whole, it depends not on itself but on explanation of the theoretical phenomena. The phrases educational theory and curricular theory may only be used in a broad and unscientific use of the word 'theory.' The science applied in the field of curricular design is based on theory of pure science, such as medical and engineering, but instead of theory it establishes guidelines to assist the decision-making in the actual conditions. Pratt's assessment on the position of theory in comprehending the process of curriculum design highlights duality between theory and practice. In his perspective, the course development is a practical phenomenon that doesn't match theory well (i.e., theory does not drive curriculum development and curriculum development does not drive theory). Pratt's conviction is that the theory alone cannot guide the curriculum.

Pratt describes design as a purposeful process in which the elements, strategies and processes of an organized learning process may be designed, planned and identified. In Pratt's view, the notion of design is a deeper collection of concepts that include the construction of both intellectual and material things. "The curriculum designer ... must create priorities to lead and carry out the choice of assignments."

Principle 2: Attitudes and beliefs on learning conceptualization

Miller and Seller (1985) propose three guidelines which are valuable and relevant to the development and understanding of beliefs and learning attitudes:

(a) Transmission Point, and

(b) the position of transformation.

Each one is useful to comprehend the philosophical, psychological and social settings of the study. The role of schooling is seen in the transmission viewpoint as conveying to pupil's information, skills and values. This approach highlights the control by traditional teaching methods and, in particular, textbook study of standard school topics. Thorndike and Skinner are the persons most identified with this perspective. The pupil is considered to be reasonable and capable of smart problem solving in the transaction situation. Education is seen as the interaction, through a dialogical process, among the learner and the student's curriculum. According to Miller and Seller, the historical history is that of the Enlightenment, with Horace Mann, John Dewey and Jean Piaget, the most prominent persons directly related to the transaction perspective. In terms of personal experience and the use of discussion in everyday life, Shor (1992) characterizes dialogue as a third language that ties to academic language. The position of transformation focuses on personal and societal change, in order to focus on ecological interdependence and the interrelation of phenomena in general. Rousseau is the historic origins of this stance. The transformation viewpoint views societal change rather than as an endeavor to control it as a movement towards harmony with the environment. The concept of pupils learning what they want to study reflects this attitude.

The principles of attitudes and beliefs may be conceptualized in the abstract pretty easily. The idea is considerably harder to implement. This idea needs to be further studied and discussed among technology teacher teachers with expertise and experience in teacher development.

Principle 3: An epistemological rationale Epistemology

During many years of education, there has been debate of the philosophy industry, which tackles origin, nature and knowledge limitations. For example, in the literature on education nowadays (Goodson, 1987) and at the turn of the century (Dewey, 1916/1966) there is a dispute over university vs utilitarian curricula. The length of the discussion testifies to the power and significance of technological knowledge as a problem.

If education cannot recognize that the basic or the initial subject in which an active work involves the use of the corpora and the handling of the material, under the influence of a scholastic conception of knowledge, which ignores all but scientifically formulated facts and truths, the subject of education is isolated from the learner and thus becomes just som. (The Dewey, quoted in 1985, pp. 65-66 in Miller & Seller). According to Miller and Seller, Dewey's points of view about issue resolution are virtually familial." Dewey says that intelligence is produced via contact between the person and the social environment, especially through resolving difficulties" (Miller & Seller, 1985, p. 65). The contrast between academic and utilitarian courses may be characterized as the difference between [academic] knowledge and knowledge that [utilitarian] can be shown or used. Learners are required to retain accurate information in educational environments (i.e., short term knowledge, through tests, exams, quizzes, or some form of recall). Do you have an opportunity to use this skill? The information necessary to carry out a particular task or project sometimes offers pupils a more comprehensive framework to understand the factual knowledge. When students perceive and internalize a need, they eventually respond to it. The experience study model (Lewin, 1975) shows the steps in the method (see Figure 1).

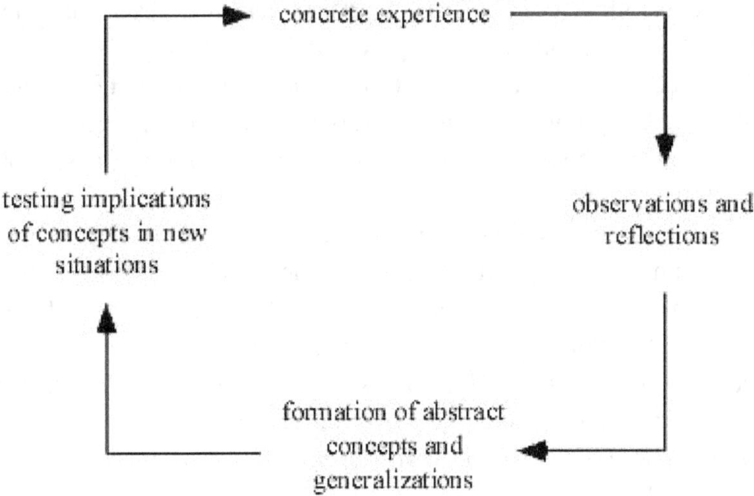

Fig 1

As a description of social learning and problem resolution, Lewin took the concept of electronics feedback as creating trustworthy data for analyzing differentiation from the desired aims. This feedback from the information provides the basis for an ongoing process of goal-oriented activity and assessment.

In the realm of technical education, formulating an epistemological justification typically demonstrates and reinforces the necessity of informing teachers explicitly about the source, nature and limits. More study is needed in order to take a proper place in the curricula of the schools in order to gain an important role for technical training.

Principle 4:

Development and planning of curricula

New instructors might be puzzled by the curriculum creation process. This procedure is typically addressed in the literature as a curriculum development plan that applies to a variety of disciplines (i. e. a macro view) but also defined as the plan for instructors to organize learning activities in the classroom (i.e., a micro view). Both curriculum development interpretations are legitimate and beneficial in designing and executing successful student education activities. With the development of a conceptual framework and a knowledge of the core of curriculum design, it is necessary for instructors to familiarize themselves with macro- and motor-level planning, the theory of learning and evaluation of students.

Principle 5: Curriculum Development Political Reality

It is an understatement to suggest that education development issues are typically extremely politized. The fact is that numerous topic groups vie for their position in school curricula in curriculum creation at the school and university level.

Their organization and curriculum material are not neutral for teacher education and, by organization, schooling. Political researchers are therefore prone to raise questions such as: Does the current focus on technology education represent a government plot to increase corporate and industrial interests, or is it a good student, school and social reform? It is important for educators to grasp the political reality to see how interest groups are competing to define the vision of a certain section of the curriculum (McCormick, 1990).

Goodson (1991), a sociologist in education, believes that curricular practice is "a complex notion, built, negotiated and renegotiated in a number of fields and levels". It's a political process, in other words. In an essay titled 'Conflicts and Crisis in Canadian Education, WothersPoon' (1987) examines the negotiation of dominant systems that infiltrated Canada's educational institutions and practices." Despite demands for democracy, 'objectivity' and 'equality of opportunity,' he suggested that schooling has continued to strengthen a highly stratified social structure along class, sex and racial lines." Educational progress in Canada, he argues, has also been marked by the struggles of different communities. According to Wotherspoon, this perspective is promoted for promoting an active and critical way of looking at the world, rather than a passive and acceptance approach: "Education in this sense involves examining the fundamental patterns of our social reality, which are underpinned to change the reality, as appropriate" (Wotherspoon, 1987).

The need for more analysis

The author has attempted to examine the development practice of curricula in technology education by identifying and defining the five principles. There have been several inquiries, some of which can lead to additional investigation, analysis and thought. The recently finished University of West Ontario technical educators (Hansen et al., 1992) research showed that rationalization of teacher curriculum creation and curriculum development is a challenge. Technology educators come from a vast array of areas with a variety of ideals. It is difficult to meet the demands of such a population. It is a dynamic process that is exacerbate the problem precisely because the curriculum is in dispute and curriculum development. It is a difficult undertaking to identify a small number of principles that can be universally used.

References

- Dogar, A., Azeem, M., Hussain, A. & Shakoor, A. (2011). Assess the development process of the curriculum. Humanities and Social Sciences International Journal, 1(14), 263-271.
- Curriculum Functions, 3(2), 161-177. Simulus, M. F. M. (1972).
- Tas, R. & Kreuzer, L. R. L. (2004). A realistic approach to the construction of curricula: a case study. Hospitality & Education Journal, 16(1), 39-46.
- Van Den Akker, J., & Thijs, A. (2009). Developing curriculum. Dutch Curriculum Development Institute (SLO).
- Hansen, R. E. Hansen (1995). Five principles to guide the construction of curricula: the instance of teaching technology.

- Ering III, J. R. & Herring III, H. C. (2000). The role of goals in the construction of curricula. Accountability Education Journal, 18(1), 1-14.

CHAPTER XXII

Analysis of Curriculum Concept, Development, Planning, and Some Improvement Recommendations

**Kaushik Debnath

• • •

Abstract

This article discusses the nature and complexity of curriculum planning from the perspective of systems theory. It argues that significant curricular change requires systems change which entails impacting change across the institutional, programmatic, and classroom levels of the curriculum. Curriculum planning for significant change thus involves the coordination of planning at all three levels, which requires a collaboration of a multitude of participants and representatives from the government, educational agencies, universities, businesses, schools, and communities at large. Providing teachers with sufficient support and resources is crucial for the planning endeavour.

This article aims also at probing into the nature of the curriculum by critically reviewing literature relevant to the term "curriculum." The multiple definitions associated with the term are inductively presented in conceptualizations so as to clarify what are the curricular issues that teachers should be concerned about in the school context. This paper then argues for the need to consider a broader spectrum of "curriculum" that embraces the whole aspects in the curriculum development process, for example, objectives, content, methodology, and evaluation of students, especially when a curricular review or evaluation is undertaken.

This article first describes three basic domains of curriculum planning which can be viewed as three constituent systems. It then discusses their interrelationships and the implications for curriculum planning for significant change. This is followed by an examination of three common models of curriculum planning which are intended to bring about significant curricular change. The article concludes with addressing what is entailed in curriculum planning for significant change.

Introduction

Nowadays, as a result of the increased evolution of scientific knowledge, and scientific openness in the world, the most important is how to use it correctly. So, the journals are the most significant sources that provide us scientific knowledge, the curriculum is considered a significant component in teaching and learning for it supplies a strategic framework to the achievement of the purposed learning results . Effective learning environment is necessary for implementing the learning process, there are many items that form a quality learning environment, and thus that the correct understanding of the learning environment, leads to adopting it is in curriculum design. So, the objective of curriculum development should be to meet the needs and requirements of the educational institution including student, teacher, and society, involving all stakeholders who participate in the educational process in curriculum development can be both a challenge and an important factor in the success of curriculum development, so still curriculum development under constant change. Curriculum development is a mechanism which goes through various stages and is implemented after every specific period defined by an educational institution concerned, an approach to develop curriculum should encompass - Designing, Selection of Content, Planning, Implementing, Strategies Methods of Teaching, Evaluating and Needs Assessment . The curriculum must be effective and adaptable to changes in the educational community. The curriculum development process needs the involvement of curriculum team in designing, planning, implementing and evaluating, Curriculum development.

Concept of curriculum

Curriculum is a contested and often misunderstood concept. At a simple level, the curriculum simply means a course of study. The word is derived from the Latin word meaning 'racecourse' or 'race', and has come to mean a general course, conveying the notion of going somewhere in a predefined direction.

However, such a conception of curriculum is obviously insufficient for understanding the complex processes of schooling in today's society. A more sophisticated definition is required, and there have been many attempts to provide one. For example, Scotland's Curriculum for Excellence states that the curriculum is 'the totality of all that is planned for children and young people throughout their education' (Scottish Government, 2008, p. 13).

Such definitions are helpful in that they broaden thinking about the curriculum and what it comprises. However, this sort of broad definition can also be confusing, as the term 'curriculum' comes to mean different things to different people. For these reasons, it is necessary to be clear about the various facets that make up the curriculum, and the ways in which these link together and interact in practice. The following terminology will all be familiar, but reflecting on it again may help to make sense of the complexity that is the curriculum.

- **Curriculum** – an umbrella term denoting the totality of the learning experience of children and young people in school. Considering the curriculum would thus include the questions of what, how and why listed below, as well as assessment.
- **Curriculum purposes** – statements of what the curriculum is intended to achieve. These include narrowly defined outcomes or objectives, and more broadly defined aims or goals. This is the 'why' of the curriculum, and is often (but not always) made explicit in official documents.
- **Curriculum framework** – the documents that outline the structure of the curriculum and its purposes. This also usually includes the content to be taught – the 'what' of the curriculum.
- **Curriculum provision** – the systems and structures established in schools to organise teaching – for example, timetabling. This is the 'how' of the curriculum.
- **Pedagogy** (often termed 'instruction' in the literature, especially in American writing) – usually referring to the teaching strategies and learning activities planned to achieve the aims and fulfil the planned framework. This is also the 'how' of the curriculum.
- **Assessment** – the methods used to judge the extent of students' learning (e.g. tests, homework, observation). Assessment judgments might be used formatively (to provide feedback to learners to inform future learning), summatively (to provide a grade) or evaluatively (to judge whether teaching has been effective).

The relationship between these elements is complex and can be problematic. I provide several examples to illustrate this point:

- The particular curriculum-planning model that is outlined in the framework can exert a major influence on pedagogy. For instance, a framework that emphasises content to be learned might encourage teacher-centred approaches to teaching, whereas a model based on processes and skills may encourage activities that are student-centred.
- The organisation of provision exerts an effect on pedagogy. For example, methods such as cooperative learning can be difficult if the school day is divided into small teaching blocks, as is the case in most secondary schools.
- A heavy emphasis on assessment can encourage narrow 'teach to the test' approaches –so-called washback.

The curriculum operates (or is made) in different ways at different levels:

- **supra** – transnational ideas about education
- **macro** – national-level policy intentions
- **meso** – policy guidance (ES, LEA)
- **micro** – school-level curricular practices
- **nano** – classroom interactions.

(Thijs and van den Akker, 2009).

Three Levels of Curriculum Planning

Curriculum planning refers to the decision-making process concerning the substance of schooling, that is, the knowledge, skills, and dispositions that constitute the experience and outcome of schooling. Broadly construed, it operates across three basic domains of curriculum; institutional, programmatic, and classroom (Doyle, 1992a, 1992b). Each of these curriculum domains constitutes a system or subsystem that, in varying degrees, has an impact on what is taught and learned in school.

- **Institutional Curriculum Planning**

The institutional curriculum embodies a conception or paradigm of what public schooling should be with respect to a society. Curriculum planning at this level is characterized by discourse on curriculum policy at the intersection between schooling, culture, and society. It invokes images, metaphors, or narratives to typify what could happen in a school or school system (Westbury, 2000). For instance, thinking School is used by the Ministry of Education in Singapore to convey a vision of schooling for the twenty-first century – a vision that defines the development of critical thinking and creativity as a central purpose of schooling. Institutional curriculum planning frames what should go on in a school or school system in terms of broad goals and general approaches to education. It serves as a means of drawing attention to educational ideals and expectations shared within a society and putting forward the forms and procedures of schooling as responses to these ideals and expectations (Doyle, 1992b: 70). Such curriculum links what is taught in schools to the social and cultural systems beyond schooling, and is always under pressure for change. Since social and cultural contexts often change rapidly, school systems always use the institutional curriculum as convenient instrument to communicate responsiveness to the outside communities (Doyle, 1992a:487).

Institutional curriculum planning is always a national or regional political undertaking. In countries with centralized education systems like France, Singapore, Malaysia, and China, the legal responsibility for institutional curriculum planning is the province of the central government. National educational bodies (ministries, departments) play a substantial role in the planning process. In countries with decentralized systems such as Canada, UK, and Australia, state or provincial governments are constitutionally responsible for making institutional curriculum decisions. Regional educational agencies are instrumental in the planning process.

- **Programmatic Curriculum Planning**

Programmatic curriculum planning is at the intermediate levels between institutional curriculum and classroom curriculum planning, with a focus on curriculum writing in the form of curriculum documents and materials (Doyle, 1992a). It translates the expectations and ideals embedded in the institutional curriculum into operational frameworks for schools, thereby bridging the gap between the abstract institutional curriculum and the (enacted) classroom curriculum (Westbury, 2000). In Singapore the notion of thinking schools becomes the introduction of thinking programs to be implemented in primary and secondary schools. The programmatic curriculum is characterized by an array of school subjects, programs, and courses of study provided to a school or a system of schools. For these school subjects, programs, and courses of study, the programmatic curriculum also spells out instructional guidance in terms of content standards, instructional frameworks, criteria for textbook approval and adoption, and assessment criteria .

- **Classroom Curriculum Planning**

The classroom curriculum, also called curriculum as event or the enacted curriculum, is characterized by a cluster of events jointly developed by a teacher and a group of students within a particular classroom (Doyle, 1992a, 1992b). It is an evolving construction resulting from the interaction of the teacher and students. Curriculum planning at this level involves transforming the institutional and programmatic curriculum embodied in curriculum documents and materials into educative experiences for students. It requires further elaboration of the programmatic curriculum, making it connect with the experience, interests, and the capacities of students in a particular classroom (Westbury, 2000). Curriculum planning can be the effort of an individual teacher or a team of teachers responsible for identifiable students, deciding alone or with students what shall occur in a specific educational setting. Such curriculum is shaped in a powerful way by a range of local factors, including teachers' own classroom perspectives, students' interests and experiences, school principals' requirements, and parents' expectations (Doyle, 1992b).

Curriculum Planning for Systems Change

As highlighted in the above discussion, the three basic p0080 domains of curriculum are interrelated and interdependent, together constituting an organic whole. Significant curricular change thus cannot be achieved by just tweaking one or two domains in isolation; it entails systems change that requires impacting change across all three domains of curriculum. To achieve this, all three levels of curriculum planning are necessary and need to work together in a way that ensures sustainable curricular change at the classroom level. A defensible model of curriculum planning for systems change, therefore, needs to take account of all three levels of planning and their relationships. None of the levels can be undermined without undermining a vital factor in curriculum planning and development. With this in mind, three common models of curriculum planning – namely top-down, bottom-up, and combination – that intend to bring about significant curricular change, or by implication, systems change – will be considered.

- **Top-Down Model**

The top-down model has been widely used in countries with a centralized education system. For many centralized countries, curriculum reform has been for a long time part of national plans and development strategies. Usually, the central government initiates curricular change by putting forward new curricular visions and goals. These visions and goals are then translated into programmatic or curricular frameworks that specify course structure, content standards, pedagogy, and assessment. Using these frameworks as a point of reference, the national education body would implement a series of initiatives such as textbook revision, assessment modification, teacher preparation, and professional development restructuring. These initiatives are expected to steer teaching and learning in classroom toward the reform visions and goals, resulting in significant change in the classroom curriculum. Also termed the framework approach (see Skilbeck, 1994), the top-down model was adopted by many traditional decentralized systems over the last two decades. For example, in the 1990s following the lead of the federal government, virtually all American states developed their state wide curriculum frameworks. In Australia, Canada, and other federated countries, there was a growing collaboration between state and federal authorities concerning the construction of an overall framework for the school curriculum based upon new curricular visions and goals (Skilbeck, 1994). These curriculum frameworks were believed to play a crucial role in steering the classroom curriculum in the reform direction.

- **Bottom-Up Model**

In contrast to the top-down model, the bottom-up model p0100 holds that significant curricular change comes from inside out rather than the outside in or from the top down. Central educational agencies (e.g., ministries of education) can really do little to influence what happens in school and classroom. To bring about change at the classroom level, curriculum planning must be grounded in the deliberative knowing and practical action of school practitioners. By participating in bottom-up approaches to curriculum planning like SBCD and action research, teachers can become the central players in the curriculum reform endeavor(MacDonald, 2003). Furthermore, a school could become a learning organization by creating conditions for school leaders and teachers to continually develop new ideas and improve their quality of thinking and capacity for reflection. They can work with students and parents to form new curricular visions, translate their visions into operational frameworks, and decide how best to bring about change in the classroom curriculum(Fullan, 1993). The assumption is that successful curricular change could be relatively easy to achieve in a local school or a cluster of local schools, and a significant number of such local changes can, over time, in an innovation diffusion process build from the bottom up into a major change in the overall educational system (Farrell, 1997).

- **Combination**

There has been an increasing interest in strengthening the relationship between curriculum planning at the national or state level and at the school and classroom level. This is based on the realization that top-down guidance and bottom-up initiatives need each other. While central educational agencies are incapable of dictating or mandating change at the school and classroom level, they still have a fundamental role to play in designing reform and translating reform into curricular frameworks, documents, and materials that could support and enable curricular change at the school or classroom level. While classroom teachers need to have sufficient freedom and autonomy in planning and carrying out curricular change, they need guidance and support provided by schools and external agencies as well. p0115 A successful combination model needs to strike a balance between top-down and bottom-up approaches. It needs to acknowledge, on the one hand, the key role of classroom teachers as curricular change agents and, on the other hand, the need for institutional and programmatic curriculum planning in guiding, supporting, and enabling curricular change at the classroom level. Three conditions are critical with respect to institutional and programmatic curriculum planning by external agencies .

Recommendations

According to content analysis, this article explained the following:

i)Curriculum development must focus on: Review of curriculum documents, Review of textbooks and other educational materials, Materials may need to be developed, Methods are to be trained and implemented, Evaluation of practice, Revision of curricula.

ii)A whole approach should be adopted for the curriculum development, and involvement of the whole staff.

iii)The studies should not only deal with the teachers or students and their perception, but also the perception of the parents, academic staff, and officials, In order to have detailed information on the design and implementation of the curriculum.

Conclusion

Significant curricular change requires systems change that entails impacting change across the institutional, programmatic, and classroom curriculum. Curriculum planning for systems change is a highly complex and challenging endeavor. It entails a coordination of institutional, programmatic, and classroom curriculum planning, the absence of any of which would not result in significant change. It requires a collaboration of a multitude of participants and representatives from the government, educational agencies, universities, business, schools, and communities at large. It needs to provide teachers with sufficient support and resources. Furthermore, it is important to bear in mind that curriculum reform is part of a larger effort to reform the school system. Curriculum planning thus needs to be related to larger issues of school change and improvement, significantly influenced by other policies and factors.

It is pertinent that we know who the individuals that affect the development of any curriculum, the curriculum developers should be knowledgeable about to plan, implement, and evaluate the curriculum, in addition, the teachers themselves are curriculum developers when they plan their classes, they are developing curriculum, briefly, curriculum development cannot be developed by one single person, it is a cooperative group work, so it is necessary the involvement of many people starting from the students, teachers community as sources for curriculum development.

References

- Cohen, D. K. and Ball, B. L. (1990). Policy and practice: A commentary. Educational Evaluation and Policy Analysis 12, 331–338.
- Akdemir, E., Karameşe, E., & Arslan, A. (2015). Descriptive analysis of researches on curriculum development in education. Social and Behavioral Sciences, 174, 3199 – 3203.
- Fullan, M. (1993). Change Forces: Probing the Depths of Educational Reform. London: Falmer.
- Fullan, M. (2003). Change Forces with a Vengeance. New York: RouledgeFalmer.

- Mohanasundaram, K. (2018). Curriculum design and development. Journal of Applied and Advanced Research, 3(1), 4-6.
- Ornsten, A. C. & Hunkins, F. P. (2013). Curriculum foundations, principles and issues (6thed). New York: Pearson .
- Tyler, W. (2013). Basic principles of curriculum and instruction. Chicago: The University of Chicago Press.

CHAPTER XXIII

Different Methodologies of Curriculum Transaction

** Mr. UdayModak,*** Mr. Chandan Maji

• • •

Introduction:

Curriculum Transaction is the effective and desired implementation of the curriculum contents on the basis of aims and objectives listed in the Curriculum. Curriculum Transaction incorporates effective planning for providing learning experiences for its learners, organization of planning and evaluation of planning, administration/implementation of the organized planning and experts in the relevant field. Curriculum, be it of the objectivist perspective or of the constructivist learning is to take place. Transaction Consists of the process of putting into practice the set of activities.

Objectives of the Study:

1. The study wills emphasis the various importance of difference Methodologies of Curriculum transaction.

2. To highlight various ways to create such an awareness about Concept of Curriculum transaction among young and future generation in our society.

3. The study will suggest the opportunities of difference methodologies of Curriculum transaction for future generation in our Nation.

4. The study will discuss about the various benefits and advantage of Curriculum associated curriculum transaction.

5. The study will conduct how we can promote the factors affecting the curriculum transaction.

Concept of Curriculum Transaction:

Curriculum Transaction incorporate effective planning for providing learning experiences for its learners, organization of planning, administration/ implementation of the organized planning and evaluation of the implementations by the implementer and the experts in the relevant field. Curriculum, be it has to a tool and it has to be transacted or implemented if learning is to take place. Transaction of a curriculum is not an easy task. It demands on the members of the teaching staff a considerable amount of reflection, visualization and planning. It calls for the maximum utilization of all available resources- physical, material, financial and human, if we wish it to be efficient and effective.

Curriculum transaction, as we have already pointed out, involves planning. In the planning process, curriculum is transformed and adapted by additions, deletions and interpretations and by decisions about place, sequence and emphasis. The process of planning and developing is to develop a step – by-step procedure for teaching that takes into account the variables of learners, resources and facilities that lead to attainment of predetermined objectives.

Factors influencing Curriculum Transaction:

As discussed above, curriculum transaction is influenced by various factors of an education system. Some of the major factors are discussed below-

1. Teacher:

As Whitaker (1979) asserts that the teachers view their role in curriculum implementation as an autonomous one. They select and decide what to teach from the prescribed syllabus or Curriculum is what teachers and students create together, as Wolfson a more significant role in designing the curriculum. Teachers must be involved in curriculum planning and development so that they can implement and modify the curriculum for the benefit of their learners.

1. Learners:

Learners are also a critical element in curriculum transaction. While teachers are the arbiters of the classroom practice the learners hold the key to what is actually transmitted and adopted from the official curriculum. The learner factor influences teachers in their selection of learning experiences, hence the need to consider the diverse characteristics of learners in curriculum transaction.

3. Resource Materials and Facilities:

No meaningful teaching and learning take place without adequate resource materials. For the officially designed curriculum to be fully implemented as per plan, the government or Ministry of Education should supply schools with adequate resource material such as textbooks, teaching aids and stationary in order to enable teachers and learners to play their role satisfactorily in the curriculum transaction process.

4. School Environment:

One other factor that influences curriculum transaction concerns the particular circumstances of each school. Schools located in rich socio-economic environments and those that have adequate human and material resources can implement the curriculum to an extent that would be difficult or impossible for schools in poor economic environment.

5. Culture and Ideology:

Cultural and ideological differences within a society or country can also influence curriculum transaction. Some communities may resist a domineering culture or government ideology and hence affect the implementation of the centrally planned curriculum.

6. Instructional Supervision:

Curriculum transaction cannot be achieved unless it has been made possible through the supervisory function of the school head "monitors and guides curriculum implementation through ensuring that schemes work, lesson plans and records of marks are prepared regularly".

7. Assessment:

Assessment in the form of examinations influences curriculum transaction tremendously. Due to the great value given to public examination certificates by communities and schools, teachers have tended to concentrate on subjects that promote academic excellence. On the other hand, on the basis of assessment we can determine the success of the curriculum and if it fails to achieve the target, it calls for modification.

Different Methodologies of Curriculum Transaction:

1. **Herbartian Model of Teaching:**

Johann Friedrich Herbart believed that new ideas, when properly presented to the students become linked to existing ideas and form a system of associated ideas. He is also known as father of scientific pedagogy. Herbart advocated five formal steps in teaching:

i. Preparation, ii) Presentation, iii) Association, iv) Generalization, v) Application.

2. **Problem solving method:**

The Child is curious by nature. He wants to find out solutions of many problems. The problem solving method is one, which involves the use of the process of problem solving or reflective thinking or reasoning. Problem solving method, as the name indicated, begins with the statement of a problem that challenges the students to find a solution. This method consists of the following steps-

i. **Identifying and defining the problem:** The student should be able to identify and clearly define the problem.
ii. **Analyzing the problem:**
iii. Formulating tentative hypothesis:
iv. Testing the hypothesis:
v. Verifying of the result or checking the result:

3. **5 E model of instruction:**

This model describes a teaching sequence that can be used for entire programs, specific units and individual lessons. Roger Bybee, developed this instructional model based on constructivism, called the "Five Es". The 5 Es represent five stages of a sequence for teaching and learning. Help the students to categorize new information in order to able to see similarities and differences between items.

4. **Asubel's theory of teaching:**

David P. Asubel is known for this theory of meaningful verbal learning and the concept of advance organizer. Asubel addresses the achievement of two broad objectives in the context of schooling, namely, - i) the long term acquisition of valid and usablebodies of knowledge and intellectual skills, and ii) the development of ability to think critically, systematically and independently. The achievement of these two goals of schooling is possible only if the classroom learning is made meaningful. He classified two types of learning-

A. Meaningful Learning
B. Rote Learning

The main elements of Asubel's model are-

I. Advance Organizer:

- Clarify aim of the lesson
- Present the Organizer
- Relate organizer to students knowledge

II. Presentation of Learning Task or Material:

– Make the organization of the new material explicit.

- Make logical order of learning material explicit.
- Present material and engage students in meaningful learning activities.

III. Strengthening Cognitive Organizer:

- Relate new information to advance organizer
- Promote active reception learning.

5. **Gagne's Instructional design:**

Gagne's work has been particularly influential in training and the design of instructional materials. Gagne's instructional theory has three major elements. First, it is based on a taxonomy, or classification, of learning outcomes. Second, it proposes particular internal and external conditions necessary for achieving these learning outcomes. And third, it offers nine events of instruction, which serve as a template for developing and delivering a unit of instruction. Gagne's identifies five major categories of learning outcomes: 1. Verbal information, 2. Intellectual skills, 3. Cognitive strategies, 4. Motor skills and 5. Attitudes.

Conclusion:

Curriculum is the crux of the whole educational process. Without curriculum, we cannot conceive any educational Endeavour. • The curriculum in a literal sense, a pathway towards a Goal. • Curriculum is actually what happens during a course i.e., lecture, demonstrations, field visits, the work with the client and so on. • Curriculum also means a written description of what happens.

▶ Curriculum is an important element of education. Aims of education are reflected in the curriculum. In other words, the curriculum is determined by the aims of life and society. Aims of life and society are subject to constant change.

Curriculum framers should used practical approach rather than ideological, reorganizing of recent curricula, solving language issue, facing controversies on curriculum change, obtaining continuous feedback and developing hearing in society at the same time. It is imperative for scholars to have effective communication skills and dynamic personality to incorporate the future trends without creating conflicts and confusion in the society. They need to know the skill to motivate and mould high ups for future changes and bring changes without development of controversies.

References:

- Dr. Jayanta Mete, Parthita iswas, Pranay Pandey-"Knowledge and Curriculum'- Rita Book
- Agency.
- Dr. Kaushik Chakrabarti & Rekheebrita Biswas-Knowledge and Curriculum- Aahali Publishers.
- Dr. Sujit Pal, Kayal Kundu, Sourovi Thakur-"Knowledge and Curriculum"-Aahali
- Publishers.
-

Author's Details

• • •

1. **Mr. Bhanumoorthy K,** *Principal (Retired from KVS), Bangalore.*

2. **Barsha Debnath,** *B.Ed Sem:- 4th Sem Trainee, Bhavan's Tripura College of Teacher Education, Narsingarh, Agartala, Dhaleswar road N-5, Agartala, Tripura(W)-799007*

3. **Dr. Abhishek Srivastava,** *Associate Professor, Faculty of Management Studies, Gopal Narayan Singh University, Rohtas, Bihar.*

4. **Divine Tomar,***Pupil Teacher, Manvi Institute Of Education And Technology, SCERT, New Delhi.*

5. **Muskan Gupta,** *Student, MBA (G), GGSIPU, Delhi.*

6. **Dr. Suprasad Lodh,** Assistant Professor, Bhavan's Tripura College of Teacher Education, Bimangarh, Narasingarh, Agartala, Tripura.

7. **Mrs. Mala Modak,** *Assistant Professor, Bhavan's Tripura College of Teacher Education, Bimangarh, Narasingarh, Agartala, Tripura.*

8. **Dr. Ekata Gupta,** *Associate Professor, Guru Nanak Institute of Management, Delhi.*

9. **Pranati Das,** *Student, B.Voc, Meerabai Institute of Technology, Delhi*

10. **Mrs.Madhurima Chaudhuri(Majumder),** Assistant Professor, Bhavan's Tripura College of Teacher Education (BTCTE), Bimangarh, Narasingarh, Agartala, Tripura,PIN: 799015.

11. **Dr. Archana S.S,** *Assistant professor, Mar Theophilus Training College, Nalanchira, Thiruvananthapuram, Kerala.*

12. **Mrs. Sanchita Mazumdar,** *Assistant Professor, Bhavan's Tripura College of Teacher Education, Bimangarh, Narasingarh, Agartala, Tripura.*

13. **Mrs. Runa Guh,** *Assistant Professor, Bhavan's Tripura College of Teacher Education, Bimangarh, Narasingarh, Agartala, Tripura.*

14. **Mr. Uday Modak,** *Assistant Professor, Bhavan's Tripura College of Teacher Education,Bimangarh, Narasingarh, Agartala, Tripura.*

15. ** **Dr. Savita Mishra,** *Principal, Vidyasagar College of Education, Phansidewa, Darjeeling, West Bengal.*

16. **Tanwangini Sahani,** *Student, MBA (G), GGSIPU, Delhi.*

17. **Ms.Rashima Sharma,** *Asst. Professor, Trinity Institute of Professional Studies, Dwarka, New Delhi.*

18. ** **Dr. Rajat Dey,** *Principal, Bhavan's Tripura College of Teacher Education, Bimangarh, Narasingarh, Agartala, Tripura.*

19. ****Mr.Suman Gupta,** *Assistant Professor, Bhavan's Tripura College of Teacher Education, Bimangarh, Narasingarh, Agartala, Tripura.*

20. ****Dr. Kotra Balayogi,***Assistant Professor, Unity College of Teacher Education, Dimapur, Nagaland – 797112.*

21. ****Krittibas Datta,** *State Aided College Teacher, Department of Political Science, Jalangi Mahavidyalaya, Murshidabad, West Bengal, India.*

22. ****Dr.Mukta Goyal,** *Principal,Manvi Institute Of Education And Technology, SCERT, New Delhi.*

23. ****Mr.Anand Prakash Dube,** *Associate Professor, School of Management Sciences, Varanasi.*

24. ****Swati Singh,** *Student, Guru Nanak Dev. Institute of Technology, Software Development, Delhi.*

25. ****Mr. K. C. Malik,** *Associate Professor(Retired), Sri Venkateswara College, University of Delhi.Director, Manvi Institute of Technology, Delhi.*

26. ** **Kanishka Tomar,** *Pupil Teacher, Manvi Institute Of Education And Technology, SCERT, New Delhi.*

27. ****Kaushik Debnath,** *B.Ed 2nd semester student, B.T.C.T.E–Bhavan's Tripura College Of Teacher Education, Narsingarh, Tripura(west), pin:- 799105.*

28. ****Mr. Chandan Maji,***Assistant Professor, Bhavan's Tripura College of Teacher Education,Bimangarh, Narasingarh, Agartala, Tripura.*

List Of Chapters And Authors' Name

www.ingramcontent.com/pod-product-compliance
Lightning Source LLC
Chambersburg PA
CBHW071937150726
47999CB00001B/237